SECRETS OF THE EUCHARIST

Secrets of the Eucharist

by

Michael H. Brown

Queenship

PUBLISHING COMPANY
P.O. Box 220 • Goleta, CA 93116
(800) 647-9882 • (805) 692-0043 • Fax: (805) 967-5843

The publisher acknowledges that since the abolition of certain Canons of the former Canonical Code, publications about new apparitions, prophecies, miracles, etc., are allowed without an express *imprimatur,* providing they contain nothing which contravenes faith or morals. Regardless, the publisher herein wishes to submit to the final judgment of the Holy See of Rome regarding any events referred to herein, including, but not limited to, claimed Eucharistic miracles or the role of the Blessed Virgin Mary and the Eucharist.

— The Publisher

Library of Congress Number 96-085387

Published by:
    Queenship Publishing
    P.O. Box 220
    Goleta, CA 93116
    (800) 647-9882 • (805) 692-0043 • Fax: (805) 967-5843

Printed in the United States of America

ISBN: 1-57918-146-5

Publisher's Foreword

The interaction between the earthly and the supernatural realms of life have always been a source of fascination for intelligent creatures dwelling in the natural world. Because the residents of Heaven, Hell, and Purgatory are unseen, it is easy for mere mortals to wonder of their existence at all.

Even more difficult, perhaps, is relating the spiritual lives and actions of God the Father, the Son, and the Holy Spirit—and all the angels, saints, suffering souls, demons, and lost souls—to our material lives. If we recall that God is spiritual, and that He is the beginning and the end—the Alpha and the Omega—of everything that is, was, or ever will be, we must first acknowledge that our own spiritual natures are fundamentally more important than our material natures. We are spiritual first, and if our lives are not focused primarily on our ethereal natures, we are missing our raison d'être. Then, too, we must face the fact that God comes first and everything else is less than Him. And He is good, and He loves us.

The most remarkable proof of God's immense love and compassion for us can be found in the Holy Eucharist. In this most Blessed Sacrament, our precious Lord, Jesus Christ, promises to be with us always. He is with us— Body, Blood, Soul, and Divinity—until the end of the world. This is a miracle.

In a previous book, *Prayer of the Warrior*, Michael Brown confronted the spiritual warfare which rages around us. Where he exposed the evil in that book, in this one, *Secrets of the Eucharist*, he presents the ultimate antidote.

Once again this best-selling author offers historical

and personal testimony which can deepen the reader's appreciation of the Holy Eucharist. He details the impressions of saints and people whose lives demonstrated serious striving for holiness.

As in years gone by, God awakens the darkened and doubtful hearts with signs and wonders, some subtle and some not so subtle. Eucharistic miracles are being reported even in our day. There are reports of visions of the Blessed Virgin Mary, encounters with angels, and statues bleeding or crying. Some of these will likely be proven true. Many will not be. But the simple fact that the reports are being made indicates that people crave a connection to the beings of Heaven.

God still longs for us, too. His call to our hearts often starts with a yearning which can be felt more than explained. A disenchantment with life grows to a sense of despair and desolation. When a soul is open, though, God will lift the veil of darkness from the soul's world-weary eyes, and He will instill an intuition of His presence and His love.

As this happens, and the soul answers the promptings of the Holy Spirit to seek God in his or her life, the tenuous reachings of the human heart become an urgent desire for a relationship with the only One Who is, was, and always will be. We are witnessing this increasingly as young and middle-aged people are returning to the Sacraments. Devotion to our Lord in Eucharistic Adoration is mushrooming at an unprecedented rate for our times. Lives are being turned around to face from whence they came, and God is there waiting and urging us forward into glory with Him. What love can this be, which tirelessly seeks His undeserving creatures? How can we be less than awed and transformed in heart?

It is our intention in publishing *Secrets of the Eucharist* that many souls be awakened to the wonderment of the most Blessed Sacrament.

Laurie Balbach-Taylor
Faith Publishing Company

Chapter 1

During the eighth century in Lanciano, Italy, a Communion Host suddenly changed into actual flesh while a doubting priest—no longer sure it was the Real Presence—was celebrating Mass. He was suddenly very certain.

During 1280 in Slavonice, Czechoslovakia, a herdsman spotted mysterious flames on a cluster of bushes. When he got there he saw a Communion Host in the middle of the fire. It was later identified as a Host that had been stolen from a local church and discarded in the area. The heat had not so much as scorched it.

In Dubna, Poland, during 1867, the devout saw soft rays glowing from a monstrance. Some claimed the manifestation was immediately followed by an image of Jesus in the Blessed Sacrament. This continued during the whole of a Forty Hour Devotion, witnessed both by believing Catholics and by schismatics who had stopped by out of curiosity.

In 1970, a red spot of blood developed on a Host in Stich, Germany. It wasn't quite as dramatic as the flesh at Lanciano, but once again it showed the Real Presence. And it was followed by dozens of similar Eucharistic miracles. In Betania, Venezuela, a priest encountered blood after he broke the large Host during Mass and the Bishop ordered it kept for special veneration. In America—the Midwest—a priest claimed that during the course of several weeks in 1996 a Host kept for ablution turned, as at Lanciano, into something resembling flesh and blood. The emotion nearly overcame him. In Upstate New York, at a shrine dedicated to Our Lady of Fatima, a medical doctor reported the sudden materialization of a

1

Communion wafer in a chapel of the Blessed Sacrament.

These are only some of the recently claimed occurrences. Many are still in need of study but already we know that, transcending boundaries, the Holy Spirit seems to be saying the same thing everywhere: I have given you signs and wonders. I have given you apparitions and healings. Now, I am showing you the True Presence.

The time has come to take the lessons we have learned from many phenomena and employ them for personal development. The time has come to join Christ's army in a more profound manner. The time has come to revisit the very cornerstones of the Catholic faith and better appreciate their power. The time has come to focus on our eternal destinations—and make sure that ours is the destination of Jesus, which means Heaven.

This is the message that comes both from Eucharistic miracles and Marian revelations.

The fruit of Our Blessed Mother is Eucharistic Adoration. She is Our Lady of the Eucharist. She was the one who gave her own flesh and blood to Jesus. She's a *part* of the Eucharist. We should remember that at Fatima, Portugal, in one of the most famous apparitions of Our Blessed Mother, the apparitions began with the appearance of an angel who held a chalice with a Host mysteriously suspended above it. The angel prostrated himself as blood fell into the cup. *"Most Holy Trinity,"* he said, *"Father, Son, and Holy Ghost, I adore You profoundly, and I offer You the most precious Body, Blood, Soul, and Divinity of Jesus Christ, present in all the tabernacles of the world...."*

At the conclusion of those famous apparitions thousands saw the sun act very strangely and what looked like a "shield" or Communion Host move in front of the solar orb, so that they could stare at it.

The Miracle of the Sun—looking as it did like a radiant Host—was another sign telling us to get back to the Eucharist.

In all the legitimate apparitions since, the common theme has been: return to the basics of the Church. Revisit the historical gifts. Understand better the sacraments. Form union with Christ not so much through the spectacular as through deeper devotion.

That's what this booklet is about, understanding the hidden power of the Eucharist, appreciating our task on earth, and deepening our fundamental devotion so that we may reach Heaven. For years I've written about apparitions of Our Blessed Mother. I've written about spiritual warfare. I've written of the evil in our era. I've written of prophecy. I've written of angels and current wonders. I can't think of more relevant topics for our special time. We're in a serious historical moment, and Mary is among us.

But when Our Blessed Mother arrives, it's always on behalf of her Son. It's always for Christ. She is the messenger of Jesus. She always points to Him. She says it's through the Eucharist and a Christian approach to life that we best come to terms with what the future has to offer. It's through the Eucharist that we understand the times in which we live. It's through Mass that we make sense of apparitions and other gifts of the Holy Spirit.

And it's through the Eucharist—through the Light of Jesus—that we dispel the current darkness.

Only if we pray and honor the sacraments will we be able to lessen events that may otherwise loom in the future.

It's an urgent and yet hopeful message.

When Christ is present, evil can not remain. When Jesus is with us, so is the Trinity. When the Trinity is with us, our very Creator is at hand. And God is infinitely more powerful than Lucifer and all the fallen angels combined!

While many of us struggle to find a way in which to lessen the illness and darkness of our world—to chase away the evil spirits—such is already available to us through Jesus and the power He set loose at the Last Supper, which was the first Eucharist.

It was at the Last Supper that Jesus took the bread, broke it, and gave it to His disciples, saying, *"This is My body to be given for you. Do this as a remembrance of Me."* He did the same with the cup of wine. *"This cup is the new covenant in My blood, which will be shed for you."*

3

They were the most powerful words since Creation. It was the denouement of Our Savior's very mission. It was a climax—a high point—of the ages. Christ was showing why He had come and the incredible nature of His rescue mission. By sharing bread and wine, the disciples would be invoking the power of His entire mission. It was a covenant meal at Passover. They would be tapping into God's power. They would be touching His garment. No wonder the ritual would survive for centuries! No wonder miracles would be associated with the Eucharist!

Henceforth, by performing the ritual Last Supper, Christians would be touching Jesus' very Heart.

When we take the Eucharist we are the bleeding woman touching the robe of Christ (*Matthew* 9:20) and feeling the healing power, and we are the wedding guests at Cana, seeing His first miracle, and we are sitting with Him as He speaks His last to the disciples.

Through the ages it has been proven that the Eucharist takes us into the New Testament. It gives us true insight. The Eucharist is where we should seek advice. The Eucharist is what guides us into the future. The Eucharist is what grants us a taste of the supernatural and sets the best path toward faith.

The Eucharist is the highest form of mysticism. For hidden in that power is the key to how we should live the current troubling times and what we can expect in the future.

Hidden in the Eucharist is the way to humility and faith.

Hidden in the Host is the key to love.

And in the Eucharist, most importantly, are the keys to Heaven.

Chapter 2

That Our Blessed Mother points to the Eucharist has been true since the very onset of the Age of Mary, which began in 1830 with the Miraculous Medal apparitions to St. Catherine Labouré. Many associate St. Catherine only with apparitions of Our Blessed Mother, but she also had visions of the Lord. She saw Him in the Blessed Sacrament. She saw His image every time she entered the chapel during the nine months of her novitiate.

Many are the saints who in Mass had such transcendental experiences. It was in the church known as San Damiano, a little, half-ruined chapel below the city of Assisi, that St. Francis had one of his greatest experiences. He used to pray before a large Byzantine crucifix that hung over the altar in that dark little structure. And his words were ones we should all adopt. "Great and glorious God, my Lord Jesus Christ!" St. Francis used to pray. "I implore Thee to enlighten me and to disperse the darkness of my soul! Give me true faith and firm hope and a perfect charity! Grant me, oh Lord, to know Thee so well that in all things I may act in Thy Light, and in accordance with Thy holy will!"

St. Francis didn't run off to gurus. He didn't seek the future in fortunetellers. He took himself to a humble church and prayed before the Cross, with fervor saying, "Speak, Lord, for Thy servant heareth!"

And that simple, faithful act was to permanently change the Church, for it was at San Damiano that a voice came from the crucifix and said, *"Now go hence, Francis, and build up My house, for it is nearly falling down!"*

The Lord was speaking not just of the chapel but of

5

the universal Church, which Francis did indeed rebuild. He exercised obedience. He had faith and listened. God speaks to us in such simplicity. He arrives in our hearts and spirits. My point is that it's in church that we should seek the supernatural. The highest form of mysticism is union with God, and the quickest way to union is through the Eucharist. Such union is not something sensational. It's not an earth-shattering vision. It's what we experience when our hearts are at peace. It's what comes after speaking silently with Jesus. It's what occurs when we detach ourselves from the world and listen to the soft, almost unspoken words that come through Communion.

As St. Catherine and St. Francis recognized, participation in Mass is participation in an actual miracle. The same perceptions were held by the great Teresa of Avila. It was during Mass that St. Teresa received the inspiration to start a convent, and once, during elevation of the Host, the saint was in such an enraptured state that she could see the Virgin on her right and St. Joseph to her left. They were clothing her with a "great whiteness and brightness" and St. Teresa felt Our Blessed Mother place a gold necklace around her neck, to which was fastened a most valuable cross.

The gold and stones were different from any on earth, their beauty beyond normal coloration.

Another time, St. Teresa saw demons on all sides but also a great light that enveloped her and prevented the devils from getting near her. It made St. Teresa realize how little power evil spirits had when she was in union with the Spirit.

She also saw Our Savior. There were many times that she had visions of Jesus. "This is so," she wrote, "especially after Communion."

The majesty with which He arrived left no doubt as to Who He was and showed, said St. Teresa, "how trifling is the power of the devils in comparison."

At Mass, that power spreads to cover all the faithful. The light of Heaven surrounds us like a bubble of bulletproof glass. *"He who eats My Flesh and drinks My Blood abides in Me and I in him,"* said Jesus (*John* 6:57).

As all the saints have stressed, He is the Bread of Life. He is the New Manna. And His Eucharist is not earthly food but the sustenance of Heaven. *"Your ancestors ate manna in the desert, but they died,"* said Christ (*John* 6:49-50). *"This is the bread that comes down from Heaven for a man to eat and never die. I Myself am the living bread come down from Heaven."*

Except that we eat the Flesh of the Son of Man, and drink His Blood, we do not have life in us. We do not have protection. But when we do, we not only have life but everlasting life. And we will be raised up on the last day. *"For My Flesh is meat indeed,"* said Jesus (*John* 6:53-56) *"and My Blood is drink indeed."*

As St. Francis de Sales once said, "In no action does Our Savior show Himself more loving or more tender than in this one, in which, as it were, He annihilates Himself and reduces Himself to food in order to penetrate our souls and unite Himself to the hearts of His faithful ones."

So precious is the Mass that saints would have eliminated everything in their lives *but* the Eucharist. They were tortured for it. They were martyred for the Eucharist. During winter Francis de Sales crawled on an icy beam of wood to cross a stream that separated him from church. He understood that Mass is the most powerful act in the universe. During Mass we are not only sitting with Christ during the Last Supper, but also walking with Him to Calvary. We are participating in His suffering. We are revisiting the Crucifixion. It's His Passion that gives the Mass its great power. We join in fellowship with the suffering, and in so doing we touch on the precious formula of salvation.

The Second Vatican Council taught that Jesus instituted the Eucharist at the Last Supper so that His sacrifice could continue throughout the centuries and across the world until His return. At Mass we are given a close view of Jesus. We are with Him more than any of His apostles were.

Think about that. Think about the fact that Mass transports us into the time of Jesus. Mass replays every event in Jesus' life and for that matter every major event leading up to it. We get this through the Gospels. We get this through other Scriptural readings. We get it through the precious Eucharistic rituals.

We relive the life of Christ with an intimacy unknown even to His closest disciples. We are with Him as God devised the plan of salvation. We are with Mary when His birth is announced. We relive the apparition of Gabriel. We are with Him at His conception. We're with Him when His power touches Elizabeth from the womb of Mary. We're with Him at His birth. We're with Him in the manger. We're with Him as He is wrapped in swaddling clothes, and when the wise men visit. We're with Him as visitors wonder at the majesty of this impoverished Infant. We're with Him when they flee to Egypt. We're with Him in Jerusalem and Nazareth. We're with Him during His major miracles.

We're with Him during the multiplication of the loaves, which was a precursor of the Eucharistic miracles.

We're with Him when He turns water into wine, when He walks on water, when He heals the sick and casts out evil spirits.

More than anything, we are with Him in the garden and then as Jesus is judged and scourged and as He carries the Cross. We're with Him as the nails are pounded into His hands, and we're with Him as He hangs on that Cross.

During Mass we're with Him as they give Him vinegar to drink. We're with Him when His side is pierced. We're with Mary and John, loving Jesus and showing Him pity as He breathes His last.

For during the Mass, during the Eucharist—as those many saints knew—we are declaring ourselves a part of His sacrifice. We're declaring a willingness to follow in His footsteps. We're acknowledging His great act of redemption. And we're declaring ourselves a part of it. We're replaying it during the liturgy. We're keeping it alive. We're saying that we will be with Jesus right through our own deaths.

That's the enormity of the power. That's the gravity of the moment. That's the transcendental nature—the truly miraculous nature—and the Eucharist.

It brings back Calvary. It keeps giving us His Blood. It defeats all sin.

As St. Thomas Aquinas once wrote, the celebration of the Holy Mass "is as valuable as the death of Jesus on the Cross."

Chapter 3

It is also as valuable as all His miracles and finally His Resurrection.

During Mass, during the Eucharist—as those many saints knew—we relive Christ's glory. As at Bethany, we receive His blessing.

We are imbued with tongues of fire.

We are sent the Holy Spirit.

And as on a cloud, we rise with Him.

We rise. We transcend. We fly above the storm clouds. We see our problems in a fuller perspective. We feel the hope of eternity.

We also feel relief from spiritual assault. Many oppressions are caused by invisible forces, but no matter how severe the attack, there is always relief in Communion. There is always a lifting of pressure.

When Satan attacks, the Host sets him back on his heels.

Let's talk about this a bit more. Let's meditate on the *power*. It's a force that is renewed at every Mass and that's why it has been around for ages. There are references to the Eucharist in frescoes dating back to the period between the first and third centuries. The same is true of Eucharistic miracles. They go back at least to a young Roman acolyte who we now know as St. Tarsicius. (Tarsicius was carrying the Blessed Sacrament to Christians in prison during a time of great persecution, and when the pagans discovered what he was doing, they beat him to death with clubs and stones—but they could find no trace of the Eucharist. It had mysteriously vanished.)

Tarsicius lived in the third century. In every century since we have seen cases where even animals have bowed before the Host, or where the Eucharist has levitated and radiated. As author Joan Carroll Cruz reports, St. Anthony of Padua once squared off with a heretic named Boniville, who rejected validity of the sacraments. Boniville denied the Real Presence. He was part of what they called the Albigensian Heresy. Anyway, it was suggested as a test of the Eucharist's real power that Boniville and St. Anthony each try to entice Boniville's mule. They would see if an animal could sense God's presence. They would deprive it of food for three days, and then Boniville would offer it food while St. Anthony offered it a Host.

They carried out the test and when Boniville tried to give the mule hay and oats, it took no notice, "but fell to its knees before the Blessed Sacrament."

The animal ignored the food of earth but not that of Heaven. In the presence of the Blessed Sacrament, it kneeled!

That same century—the 13th century—there was a miracle at Santarem, Portugal, about 35 miles from present-day Fatima. There a Host was stolen from a church by a woman who was following the directions of a sorceress. She took it from her mouth after Communion and hid it in a veil, but as she tried to leave, the Host began to bleed. The blood soaked into the cloth. It caused an obvious stain. She certainly didn't want anyone to see it. So she hurried home and hid it in a chest.

During the night, however, as she tried to sleep, the cloth caused a mysterious light to issue from the chest, illuminating the whole house. She and her husband a-dored the miracle until the dawn hour!

Such events are given to us in order to make sure we understand the Eucharist's hidden power. They are given as evidence of the Real Presence. Those who were wise, those who had spiritual insight, already appreciated it. St. Ignatius of Loyola, who founded the Jesuit Order, was one who knew the power, who had proper reverence. He required an hour to prepare for Mass—that's the importance he attached to it—and while standing at the altar he often fell into deep, coma-like raptures.

During one such ecstasy a flame appeared above his head, and when another priest rushed to extinguish it, he realized St. Ignatius was lost in contemplation and unaffected by the "fire."

Meanwhile, during Mass at Assisi, Italy, Brother John of Alverna, a disciple of St. Francis, encountered the actual sight of angels. He saw the heavenly entities. He saw the spirits who are usually invisible but who come in great multitudes during Mass. Brother John almost fainted at their grandeur. He was probably awed at how, during Adoration, they took majestically to their knees.

Once, he did collapse, unable to bear the great majesty of Jesus. He saw Christ enter into the Host at the finish of the consecration. The bread vanished and Brother John actually witnessed the Lord incarnate and glorified. So rapt in ecstasy was Brother John that he was carried into the sacristy as if dead!

Other saints levitated when they communicated, or a mysterious light brightened their faces—just as a light shone on the face of Moses after he had encountered God (*Exodus* 34:29).

There have been Communion Hosts that suddenly materialized on the tongues of saints, or mysteriously multiplied. There have been claims throughout the century of Hosts reproducing like the loaves of bread. It's said that one time St. John Bosco was serving Mass to a large gathering of 600 boys. It was the feast of the Nativity of the Blessed Mother. There were hundreds there but when Bosco looked in the ciborium, there were only about twenty hosts.

Gazing heavenward, Bosco called for a miracle. He implored God's grace. And ignoring that limited supply, he then began freely distributing the Eucharist. He acted like everything was all right. He acted as if there were an unlimited supply. He operated with blind faith.

And one after another, row after row, the young men received their Hosts. Every single one received. Not a boy was left without. There were plenty of wafers. And afterward, there were even some left over!

Such a reflection reminds us that Mass is not just a prayer meeting. It's not just a gathering of the faithful. It's a confluence of supernatural forces. It transcends the physical. At Mass the powers of Heaven—the greatest angels and saints—are in Adoration. There is heavenly presence. There is presence from unseen cherubs. There is presence from all the saints. Only after we die, when we see with spiritual eyes, will we realize all that transpires at Mass.

St. Teresa described how the power bestowed upon us by Our Lord is such that demons cower. They're terrified when we're in a state of grace. They're horrified at Mass, in which we glow with God's power.

St. Teresa saw it in the visions which so often occurred during the Eucharist. She saw it during her famous ecstasies. "If this Lord is powerful, as I see He is, and know He is, and if the devils are His slaves (and of that there can be no doubt, for it is an article of the Faith), what harm can they do to me, who am a servant of this Lord and King?" she asked. "How can I fail to have fortitude enough to fight against all Hell?"

When Jesus is in our hearts—which is where the Eucharist brings Him—demons, said the saint, are no more powerful than insects.

Chapter 4

There are angels at Mass and there are saints. There is Joseph. There is the Blessed Virgin, whose statue is so often near the tabernacle.

But above all, there is Jesus.

Above all, there is the Redeemer.

A priest in Northern Ireland once wrote that if you took all the bishops, priests, and religious now on earth, along with millions of the faithful and all the saints in Heaven and the souls in Purgatory—all the millions of angels also—and watched them bow in Adoration before God, however incredible that would be, however much glory it would give God, still this would be less than a single liturgy.

"And why?" he wrote. "Because in the Mass it is not angels and saints alone who pray for you; it is Jesus Christ Himself, and He not only prays for you but He also offers up His merits for you, and as He is God, His prayers and His merits give infinitely more glory to God and are infinitely more powerful than the united prayers and offerings of all the angels and men, even if they were continued for all eternity."

There have been saints who spent hours—entire mornings and afternoons—just to thank God for that day's Eucharist.

There was even a saint who said two Masses a day: one the regular morning liturgy and then a Mass in thanksgiving for the previous one!

We don't need a miracle to know the Mass's value. We don't have to see visions to appreciate the Eucharist. We feel it. We live it. We receive its graces. Father Stefano Manelli, an Italian priest who wrote an invaluable little

booklet, *Jesus Our Eucharistic Love*, from which I have
drawn material, points out that Holy Communion "is of
much greater value than an ecstasy, a rapture, or a vision. Holy Communion transports the whole of paradise
into my poor heart!"
From the tabernacle comes the fragrance of Heaven.
Without it, the saints felt themselves shrink. They
hungered. They felt left out. One day St. Anthony of
Padua was confined to his cell and unable to assist at
Mass—which greatly distressed him. He wanted to be
there. He longed to see the Host elevated. It was torture
to be away from the Mass, and so when the monastery
bell rang, signaling elevation of the Host and chalice, he
instinctively fell to his knees.
That's when it happened: the wall of his cell suddenly
"opened" and he could see right through it.
He could see into the church. He could see the altar.
He could see the priest. He could see the Sacred Host!
There were witnesses who attested to it. So intense was
his desire that God allowed him to miraculously partake
of the Sacrifice, even at a distance.

The Mass meant so much to St. Thérèse the Little
Flower that she treated her First Communion as most
women would recall their weddings.
"The smallest details of that heavenly day have left
unspeakable memories in my soul!" wrote St. Thérèse.
"The joyous awakening at dawn, the respectful embraces
of the teachers and our older companions! The large room
filled with *snow-white dresses* in which each child was to
be clothed in her turn! Above all, the procession into the
chapel and the singing of the morning hymn: 'O altar of
God, where the angels are hovering!'"
The second time she received was just as sweet, because with Communion, Thérèse now understood, it was
no longer that *she* lived but that Jesus lived through her.
During Communion, He enters us; He becomes a part of
us. He possesses and consumes us.
The power of that very statement was enough to cause
saints like Philip Neri to fall into ecstatic states.
Masses offered by St. Philip often lasted two hours or
more, and the same was true of Padre Pio. In books about

the famous Italian mystic, who died in 1968, we learn of his extraordinary appreciation of the Mass, during which he seemed to suffer the very Passion of Jesus. As biographer C. Bernard Ruffin wrote, within Mass "Padre Pio admitted to an intense mystical involvement with the unseen world. He apparently saw, as in a vision, the entire Passion, and actually felt, physically, the wounds of Jesus. When he read the Epistle and Gospel of the day's Mass, he identified so closely with their content that he frequently would shed copious tears. During the offering of the bread and wine, Padre Pio often remained motionless for moments on end, as if 'nailed by a mysterious force,' gazing with moistened eyes upon the crucifix."

Pio suffered the most during the Consecration, when he felt the horrible weight of all sin—as well as the enormity of God's unmerited affection.

It was said by Padre Alessio Parente, who assisted Pio for three years, that more people were touched by Padre Pio's Masses than by his thousands of cures, bilocations, visions, and prophecies. For during Mass they felt the very reality of Calvary—where the most powerful event since creation occurred—and it seemed as if Padre Pio's very facial features transfigured into those of Our Savior.

During Mass Pio took what seemed like endless pauses, meditating on the power of what he was doing and so identifying with Christ's suffering that he was barely able to speak the liturgical words.

Like St. Philip's, the Masses were long affairs even though Pio did not deliver a homily!

Afterward he appeared exhausted and leaned over the altar for several minutes as if in further conversation with the Lord.

One can thus sense the immense power. One can realize that Mass goes far beyond ritual. One can see that it delivers in proportion to what we invest in it: that there is no prayer as powerful, no act so sublime, and no action on earth more precious.

"If you would know what grace and what gifts you receive, you would prepare yourselves for it each day for an hour at least," Our Blessed Mother told the seers at Medjugorje. *"Let the Holy Mass be your life. I wish that the Holy*

Mass be for you the gift of the day. Attend it, wish for it to begin. Jesus gives Himself to you during Mass. Thus, look forward to that moment when you are cleansed. The Mass is the most important and the most holy moment in your lives. Mass is the greatest prayer of God. You will never be able to understand its greatness."

Chapter 5

It's during Mass that God most closely listens. It's then that our prayers pierce the clouds. It's when our prayers are most powerful.

Why is that?

Because we are honoring His Son and participating not just in the joy but also in Calvary.

The key to the joy of Heaven is the Passion.

It is in the suffering that love is proven.

"Let not My friends then tremble as if abandoned when tribulation comes upon them," Jesus told St. Bridget. *"My Father wishing to show the way by which Heaven should be opened and excluded man enter in, out of love delivered Me up to the Passion, that by accomplishing it, My body might be glorified. For in justice, My humanity could not enter glory without passion, although I might have done so by the power of My divinity."*

Knowing that, we should always prepare for the Sacrifice. We should treat every Mass as a precious opportunity. We should see it as a portal to Heaven. We should always pray on the way to Mass. We should recite a Rosary before the liturgy, or at least make a strong mental prayer, imploring the Holy Spirit. We should also offer up our special intentions. This should be done, actually, at the very start of every day. It's crucial to pray for at least 15 minutes in the morning to clear the nighttime debris. We should make requests for family and friends and we should repeat or add requests during elevation of the Eucharist, for when the priest is holding Christ aloft, after the Host has been consecrated, Christ manifests His greatest Presence.

In a gentle way, without hyperbole, the air becomes

rarefied.

During elevation Jesus is most closely listening. It is at that moment that He rises and breaks through the strongholds of evil. It is then that Light overcomes dark and we see hope where before we saw misery.

As it says in 2 *Thessalonians* 1:9, the wicked can not stand in Jesus' Presence. Devils are in torment. They howl and scream! For during Mass their power is broken—they are forced to take flight—and we begin to feel an inner healing.

If we are sick and it's God's Will that we be healed, that healing may well begin at the Eucharistic moment.

If we're sad, we feel happiness.

If we're depressed, God arrives to lift oppression.

During Mass God's ear is especially open to any form of anguish.

There's such a remarkable feeling that sometimes it seems the Host will actually glow as it has during so many Eucharistic miracles. Peace comes over the congregation, especially when the Host is aloft for a long moment. Especially when the priest treats the moment with special reverence. *Imp.*

They say Padre Pio would elevate the Host for a full five minutes and that it was during this time that his face would transfigure into the face of Our Savior.

During elevation all powers vested to a priest suddenly precipitate. The powers are realized. Through the priest's consecrated fingers comes a flow of the Holy Spirit, and no one but a priest can mediate such a moment.

Only a priest can consecrate. The consecrated hands are of overwhelming and yet little appreciated importance. When the Host is held aloft, you can nearly feel the presence of those many saints and angels. You can nearly see Christ's Face in the large wafer. There is a hush and also a sensation of tranquility. The Prince of Peace has arrived. He has entered. He is with us. How many saints have bodily levitated during Mass, showing us yet again the power that's available?

One day while Pope Celestine V was celebrating Mass onlookers were astonished to see him surrounded by light and elevated in the air. The same happened to St. Alphonsus Liguori and St. Angela Merici. Others like Joseph of Cupertino would go as high as twenty or more feet.

It reminds us that God transcends all physical laws. It reminds us of Jesus resurrecting.

It reminds us that through faith Christ could even walk on water.

And it reminds us that first and foremost the Mass is a miracle.

Others see Him. The famous mystic of Divine Mercy, Sister Faustina Kowalska of Poland, had a vision of a cenacle in which, before the Consecration, she saw Jesus with His eyes to Heaven. He was in a mysterious conversation with the Father. "His eyes were like two flames," she wrote in her diary. "His face was radiant, white as snow; His whole personage full of majesty, His soul full of longing. At the moment of Consecration, love rested satiated."

What a moment for us to lift our hearts with wants and needs! What a moment to make yet additional supplications, as well as send our greatest love to Jesus! It's during Communion that we should lift up our heartfelt petitions because suddenly Jesus is in us and is permeating us and we are just what it says: in *communication*.

I'm not speaking about locutions or voices from a cloud but about the special nonverbal way in which we reach union with Jesus.

Heart to heart.

Spirit to spirit.

Chapter 6

The same is true of the Blessed Sacrament. Kneeling in Adoration is worth more than anything. It's worth more than any other human effort. It's better than writing a book or starring in a movie. It's better than receiving the Nobel prize or running for governor. It's certainly more valuable than anything money can purchase. It's more precious than sitting on a yacht or sleeping in a Palm Beach mansion. For that matter, it's more majestic than sitting on the throne of England.

Maximilian Kolbe used to visit the Blessed Sacrament ten times a day. That's the value he saw in it. The same was true of Padre Pio, who once said, "A thousand years of enjoying human glory is not worth even an hour spent in sweetly communing with Jesus in the Blessed Sacrament."

Mass and the Blessed Sacrament share the same history. As I said, the first Eucharist commenced at the Last Supper, and afterward early Christians practiced a meal of ritual character. They prayed and broke bread while they remembered Jesus.

By the middle of the second century the sacramental meal had become an independent rite, celebrated in conjunction with reading and preaching on Sunday morning. What we know today as the Mass was standardized in the period between the emperor Constantine in the fourth century and Pope Leo the Great, who died in 461. We are thus talking about a practice that is 2,000 years old and was directly inspired by Our Savior.

While there have been many changes in those 2,000 years, the essence of Mass has remained an invocation of Christ's power. It's the complete prayer. And it often starts with commemorating the dead, which is something I'll speak about later when we discuss Purgatory. For now, suffice it to say that souls in Purgatory would give *anything* to be able to attend just one earthly Mass, now that they understand its tremendous underpinning. A single Mass can help a purgatorial soul unimaginably!

But like I said, we'll discuss that at greater length later.

The dedication of the Mass is followed by the priest invoking the Holy Spirit. This is crucial because it is the Holy Spirit Who gives all gifts, Who empowers all grace, and Who thus should be invoked not just during Mass but on the way to Mass and much of the time we're sitting in the pews.

Nothing comes from Heaven without empowerment by the Holy Spirit, and when we invoke Him, He opens our spiritual eyes. He grants us knowledge we could never attain by ourselves. And it's the Holy Spirit Whose presence is detected in a strong feeling of peace and grace.

The Holy Spirit is grace. When He comes during Mass, right there at the beginning, it reminds us how the dove descended from Heaven and alighted on the head of Jesus when He was being baptized at the very beginning of His public ministry. It's the Holy Spirit that empowers the priest and blesses him in a similar way. Priests are extremely powerful. Priests are standing in for Jesus. And that's why Satan so often attacks them. They have hands and fingers that are *consecrated*. I would rather be touched by the blessed hands of a priest than any visionary or mystic.

I recall the account of a friend of mine who in 1992 had the tremendous privilege of sitting in at a meeting between the famous Fatima seer Lucia dos Santos and former President Corazon Aquino of the Philippines.

My friend told me that President Aquino had come to Portugal with a bag or two full of religious items. She wanted Sister Lucia to "bless" them.

The visionary was taken aback. Bless an object? No, said Sister Lucia; she could never bless *anything*. Only a priest could bless such items, and she referred them to a humble priest who was there serving as a translator.

We should share that appreciation. A priest's hands are miraculous. They have real powers. It's said that at night the thumbs and index fingers of a priest named Conrad of Costanza, who was a saint, used to shine as an indication of the faith and love with which he handled the Eucharist. It's those same hands that bless us at the beginning of Mass as Jesus blessed near Bethany.

After the priest leads us in blessing, we invoke an indwelling of the Holy Spirit. We also acknowledge our failures and sins. The priest asks us to recall our transgressions, and when we do, when we conscientiously admit to our mistakes—large and small alike—we shake loose the grit of evil, because to acknowledge a fault or sin can be to rebuke and bind a sin—which also means rebuking Satan.

It's very important to boot Satan out of our way before we get into the deeper aspects of Mass, because otherwise he tends to divert or harass us, especially in our present time, when demons are so numerous and flagrant. Scripture compares this to binding a "strong man" (*Matthew* 12:29) and tells us that whatever is bound on earth *"shall be bound in Heaven"* (*Matthew* 16:19).

In so doing, we also implore God's Mercy. That's one of the most important and forgotten aspects of Christ: His Mercy. This is extremely significant, because as Sister Faustina said, God expresses His love in a most powerful fashion through His Mercy.

God's Love is His Mercy. We should invoke it and take refuge in it and know that when we seek mercy we are automatically dispelling evil influences.

In the very first minutes of Mass, we are thus blessed by the priest, we have invoked the Holy Spirit, we have repudiated evil influences, and we have tapped into the powerful force of mercy. God's Mercy is something we seek at several points during Mass and is an essential ingredient of the liturgy. *"Proclaim that mercy is the greatest attribute of God,"* Jesus told Sister Faustina. *"All the works of My hands are crowned with mercy. I desire the whole world know My infinite Mercy. I desire to grant unimaginable graces to those souls who trust in My Mercy. The flames of mercy are burning Me. I desire to pour them out upon human souls. Tell aching mankind to snuggle close to My merciful Heart, and I will fill it with peace. Tell all people, My daughter, that I am Love and Mercy itself."*

Those are composite quotes that summarize much of Sister Faustina's potent message, and they always draw back to the Eucharist, for it's during Communion that we "snuggle close" to His Heart. When we do, when we approach Him with trust, He further promises to fill our souls with such an abundance of graces that we cannot contain them all and thus we radiate them to others.

That's why, after Mass, we feel clean and "white." We are radiating. Grace is flowing in and out. I often glance at people who regularly attend the Eucharist, especially older women who have been going to daily Mass for many years, and I often notice a radiant *cleanliness* around them. They're actually radiant.

It's just such a radiance that serves as the best protection against evil spirits.

During Holy Mass Sister Faustina felt enveloped by a "great interior fire." She felt "all aflame." That's because the divine floodgates are open when we attend Mass with trust and seek God's Mercy. "Jesus, I believe in You," we should say during the first part of the Mass. "Jesus, I plead Your Blood. I plead Your Life. I plead Your Word."

That should lead up to the readings from the Bible, which are also so important in drawing down grace.

Indeed, digesting elements of Scripture leaves us with the same sweet grace as we sense during recitation of novenas or the Rosary.

During Mass we hear from both the Old Testament and the New Testament, and if you go to Mass every day, you hear just about the entire Bible every three years. On Sundays there are three readings, first from the Old Testament, then from the writings of the apostles, and third from one of the Gospels.

After a homily, the priest then gets down to the all-important business of leading up to the Consecration. We are lead to praise and thank God. We are lead to fully acknowledge Christ's Godhead. We are taken to a re-enactment of the last Supper, and as such we become as close to Him as the disciples.

"Blessed are You, Lord, God of all creation," says the priest. "Through Your goodness we have this bread to offer, which earth has given and human hands have made. It will become for us the bread of life."

And the people respond: "Blessed be God forever."

At Mass, we're in the Upper Room. We're with Jesus. The Eucharist we take is as real as the bread He broke. It too has been touched by Him. It is imbued with His Spirit.

Before the priest elevates the chalice, he pours a little water into the wine, which one scholar says is a rite with roots in an old custom—perhaps adhered to by Christ at the Last Supper—of drinking wine only after it had been mixed with water.

But more important is the symbolism. It symbolizes the "blood and water"—actually blood and then thinner fluid devoid of serum—that flowed from Jesus' side wound during the Crucifixion.

Some consider this event—the emanation of blood and water—as representing the very birth of the Church and its sacraments. It unites the human with the Divine. It bridges the flow of the supernatural with raw physical existence. It puts us in the presence of heavenly spirits. "By the mystery of this water and wine may we come to share in the divinity of Christ," says the priest, "Who humbled Himself to share in our humanity."

What could have shown more humility than God manifesting as a human? His descent was the ultimate act of modesty and unselfishness. And His blood, like the Passover blood, was the Blood of the Lamb that keeps away the avenging angel. This is why it can be beneficial to partake of the cup during Communion. When we are marked with His Blood, we are under a special protection.

When we drink His Blood, we do so as with the angel of Fatima.

Chapter 7

That's right. During Mass we're part of the heavenly court. We're surrounded by angels.

Back a couple years ago I received a letter from a woman who lives in Minnesota. I get many letters, but this one touched me. She sounded very level-headed and recounted how, in 1986, during Consecration of the Eucharist, "I looked up and all of a sudden I could see with my physical eyes a multitude of adoration angels, suspended in a devout posture, encircling the altar, adoring the Eucharist—Jesus. Their presence enhanced the devotion to God within my own heart. At the very moment of Consecration, several angels were lying prostrate at the foot of the altar. I noticed every single adoration angel positioned lower than the Eucharistic Host as Father held it up for all to praise and take notice of. Many were dressed in light, translucent gowns of heavenly colors shown in pinks, aqua, yellow, blue, and green, bathed in light. I was given the knowledge that these are adoration angels and their place before God is to adore the Eucharistic Jesus during Mass and they are always present during Consecration."

I have spoken to others and read historic cases that bear the vision out: During Mass, there is tremendous supernatural activity. The church is full of heavenly spirits. Especially present are the Blessed Virgin. St. Joseph, and the Archangel Michael, who is the Church's protector. And the other angels. The countless angels. The angels just as there were angels present at Christ's birth and His trial in the desert. Angels just as there were angels at His tomb after the Resurrection. They remind us that Jesus is special. He is not to be looked upon as just a historical figure. He exists at the spiritual plane and as such is closer to us than ever.

Christ is Spirit. He is everywhere all at once and sends forth special blessings—His incomparable Presence—when we do what He told us to do and partake of the Eucharist.

"For I shall see you again, and your hearts will be full of joy, and that joy no one shall take from you" (*John* 16:22).

It's during Mass that we "see" Him. It's during the Eucharist that we are most closely in touch with Him. It's during Mass that a window is opened to the spiritual dimension—and we are surrounded with the same light, the same joy, that Sister Faustina and St. Teresa of Avila felt enveloping them.

During Mass God's power manifests itself in a living light, a life-giving, joyful light that serves as the extreme opposite and antidote of darkness.

It arrives to give us peace when we seek to do God's Will and when we love with a pure heart.

That's how Christ appears: as Light. That's how He came to Saul. We glimpse this light with angels. It's the same kind of illumination that surrounds God's messengers. Recall in Scripture (*Matthew* 28:3) that in appearance one angel *"resembled a flash of lightning while his garments were as dazzling as snow."* When Jesus ascended into Heaven, there were angels once again, *"dressed in white"* (*Acts* 1:10), and His very Ascension, when He lifted on a cloud before the eyes of His apostles, reminds us of how His mother later arrived on a cloud at Fatima and Medjugorje.

But at Mass we're at a higher level than a visionary. Our communication is more profound than what occurs even during an authentic apparition. We are not communicating with our minds. We're not usually seeing with our eyes, or hearing with our ears. We're communicating from the depth of our souls and hearts.

And we're communing with Christ.

It's no surprise that at places such as Medjugorje, pilgrims have reported seeing the altar turn into bright lights or appear as if the priests were standing on heavenly clouds. It's no wonder people have seen saints and angels. It's no wonder that in church they have seen floating hearts.

We may not see flashes of light, we may not hear voices from a cloud, we may not even sense angelic spirits, but one day, looking back from Heaven, we'll see that such a reality is more real than the physical world, and that we can truly touch that reality when we receive the Eucharist. Christ's power flashes upon us. And the priest becomes His proxy. As a great theologian named Adolphe Tanquerey once wrote, "Each and every priest is, strictly speaking, a secondary minister of the Sacrifice of the Mass. Christ Himself is the principal minister."

Recall again that after His Resurrection, during His apparitions to the apostles, Jesus *"led them near Bethany, and with hands upraised, blessed them. As He blessed, He left them, and was taken up to Heaven"* (Luke 24:50-51).

This is now the priest's job: to take us near Bethany. He blesses us. He blesses us at the very beginning of Mass. He blesses us to set the Holy Spirit flowing. He blesses us to wash away the grit of the world. He blesses us to protect us from evil spirits. He blesses us to bring us health and holiness.

Wholeness.

When a priest blesses us, he is doing so to invite the Trinity and to dispel evil spirits.

Padre Pio once explained this to a woman in the confessional booth and the woman was horrified.

Demons! Was he saying she was possessed?

It was more a case of deliverance, and at various times we all need deliverance. "I did not dispel the devils *out* of you," he replied, "but *away* from you."

Confession and the Eucharist do this in the same way that soap cleans a sink. They expel spiritual dirt and keep evil spirits from affecting us with oppression and temptation.

We also bless ourselves. Our very entrance into church should be signaled by making the Sign of the Cross with holy water, which immediately reminds us of our baptismal cleansing. Holy water is tremendously powerful in chasing away evil spirits because the water reminds us of our Baptism, and the sacrament of Baptism includes a rite of exorcism. It also brings to mind the water that flowed from the side of Christ during His Crucifixion.

Entering church, we are thus renouncing sin and opening ourselves to the renewal of baptism. Demons hate this. They hate it when we bless ourselves. And certainly they hate when the priest, with his special hands, blesses us during Mass. They detest our blessing ourselves just before the priest reads from the Gospels. You can nearly hear their screams and howls. They hate the threefold blessing, whereby we seal our foreheads and hearts and mouths. They hate when we seal ourselves by receiving the blessing at the end of Mass. For when we bless ourselves we are not just shaking off the grime of evil but invoking the Father, Son, and Holy Spirit to pervade our bodies and spirits.

When we have the Holy Spirit, when we are filled with Him, there's no room for a demonic presence.

Although many don't like to discuss it, the influence of demons is ignored only at our own peril. If we could see the many effects of demons, we'd be both surprised and appalled. They cause many emotions that we usually attribute to just a "bad" day or an emotional hangup. They cause imbalance. They especially cause negativity. They cause anxieties to wing into our brains, or they cause us to become obsessed and angry. They cause us to dwell on unpleasant failings. They seek to set us against each other and imbue us with their pride and superior attitude.

At Mass that pride is broken by the humility of Jesus. The importance of humility was demonstrated when Jesus rose from the Last Supper, poured water into a basin, and began to wash the feet of His disciples. They were naturally shocked that their Teacher and Lord would stoop to such a thing! But Jesus explained that humility was His heritage, and He instructed them to do likewise, washing each other (*John* 13:15). He did this before indicating that Judas was a traitor. He did this before confronting evil, which shows us the power of humility over pride. He did this before confronting His death and returning to the Father.

Jesus knew that only if we have pride can Satan have

a legal claim to any of our spiritual territory. He knew to defeat the devil He needed humility. Satan is the prince of pride and thus lord of vain emotions. When we exhibit pride, he is invoked. He is allowed to come. He takes a little piece of us, and then another piece, until he is able to cause us trouble.

Humility divorces us from the influence of Satan and leads us, as during the washing of feet, to tender and self-less acts of love.

Love is itself a selfless emotion, a giving away of one-self, and that's precisely what Christ was celebrating at the Last Supper: His humble love.

He knew He was going to die, but His faith was like iron. His faith had joined as a powerful force with humili-ty and love.

These form the crucial triumvirate of spiritual exis-tence.

They are the three deepest secrets of the Eucharist and they are the way we defeat Satan: faith, humility, and love.

Chapter 8

The formula of salvation was thus given at the Last Supper. Pray. Have faith. Love as Jesus loved. Be as humble as Christ was when He washed the feet of His disciples.

This, it is indicated, will lead to a pleasant afterlife.

This is the safest way. The narrow gate.

Serve others. Serve God. Praise God. Love your Creator with all your heart.

Love the Trinity. Love the Holy Spirit. Love Christ.

If you do nothing else in life, love well. Love and suffer well. Love as Jesus loved on the Cross.

Praise Him every day. Praise the Lord. When we praise and adore God, when we glorify Jesus, when our love is proven by how we endure our trials, we are invoking God in the most powerful fashion and can feel the peace of His love.

That's the essential message of the Gospels, and it comes to life during the Eucharist. It comes to life when we adore God by starting Mass with a responsorial psalm. I don't think there are many prayers superior to the praises in *Psalms*. *"Praise the Lord in His sanctuary,"* say the final ones. *"Praise Him in the firmament of His strength. Praise Him for His mighty deeds, praise Him for His sovereign majesty. Praise Him with the blast of the trumpet, praise Him with lyre and harp, praise Him with timbrel and dance, praise Him with strings and pipe. Praise Him with sounding cymbals, praise Him with clanging cymbals, let everything that has breath praise the Lord!"*

I remember when I returned to an active Catholic faith how powerful it was to thank and praise God. God is worthy of all praise and thanks. He is so good! He is so merciful! Suffering is nothing compared to eternal joy.

How can we thank Him enough for the afterlife? How can we thank Him enough for eternity? With Christ, joy is always the end result. Calvary is the door to Resurrection. When there is attack and oppression, when there are concerns and obsessions, when there is anxiety, a litany of praise—whether read from the *Psalms* or in spontaneous prayer—is immediately comforting. Such prayers take on all the more force when said before the Blessed Sacrament. Many were the saints who spent hours at a time—literally ten or twenty hours—in front of the Blessed Sacrament, enraptured with Heaven, adoring God. They didn't notice anything in the chapel but the Blessed Sacrament. You could have taken the stoles from their shoulders or raised a din and they would not have taken much notice. They were in the reality of Adoration. And that's why they were so free of evil. Just as he can't remain in the presence of love and humility, neither can the devil remain within earshot of praises to God.

The rays from the Eucharist are arrows against the wiles of Satan.

During prayer and Mass we should thank God not just for the small favors of life, not just for the new job, or the answered prayer of a family member, or for help during illness, or for those thousands of other things we ask for, but for life itself. Mass should be one huge display of gratitude for the very fact of *existence*. It should be a feast of thanks. It should be an acknowledgement. No matter how trying life can become (it's meant as a test), we should always remember that it's followed by eternity. How can we ever thank God enough for creating us in the first place? How could there ever be sufficient gratitude? Nowhere does God show His love so heartily as through the very fact that He created us and allows us to share His Kingdom.

Think about this. Think about this when small troubles hound you. Think of the fact that out of nothing God created your spirit and through the soul manifested it into an earthly body.

After earthly life, it will ascend for all time to the spiritual. *"You may be sure,"* the Lord told St. Gertrude, *"that regarding one who devoutly assists at Holy Mass, I will send him as many of my saints to comfort him and protect him during the last moments of his life as there will have been Masses which he has heard well."*

How can we even comprehend such generosity? If you started to praise God from the very moment of conception and praised Him every waking second for the rest of your life, you would still be praising Him but a little.

Only through infinite generosity did He form us out of what would otherwise have been sheer nothingness.

When we look at it that way, when we see it in the light of eternity, our prayers of thanksgiving flow from the heart. No longer is the responsorial psalm something we repeat like robots. Inside, we feel appreciation and indebtedness. When we contemplate how God not only created us, but then has endured our shortcomings and sent His only begotten Son to suffer for them, our minds our boggled at how He could conceivably put up with us.

During Mass, we live through the birth of Jesus, His life, His death, and His Resurrection, all the while acknowledging the beneficence of God.

And when we meditate on His goodness, as evidenced through the Resurrection, we are in touch with His Spirit, which transcends time and space and pervades all the universe.

Chapter 9

The awesomeness of God is realized when we contemplate stars and planets. The earth is less than a hundredth the size of the sun, and the sun is 93 million miles away—so far that it takes a beam of light traveling at about 185,000 miles a second more than eight minutes to reach us.

That huge orb of heat and light is tremendous to us, but in the larger scheme of our galaxy, it's a grain of sand. The sun is but a star and there are hundreds of billions of stars in the Milky Way alone, many far larger than our sun. It takes not minutes or even hours but *years* for the light from the closest star to hit earth.

When you look up at the stars at night, remember that not a single one is really where you see it. What you're seeing is where that star was many years or centuries ago!

And imagine how many other planets there are circling the stars in our galaxy!

Then realize that the Milky Way, huge as it seems, spreading for a diameter of 100,000 light years, or 588,000,000,000,000,000 miles, is only one of endless *galaxies*. Our galaxy itself—those thousands of trillions of stars in the Milky Way—is but a larger grain of sand. At the speed of light it would take many thousands of years to reach the end of the next galaxy, and millions of years to skirt the outer reach of the universe, if indeed there *is* a limit to the universe.

Now, consider the fact that if you could get to the farthest reach of the galaxies, on the very most distant planet—somehow out there in the blackest part of space—you would still find God.

You would still find the Holy Spirit and Christ.

These distances are nothing to One Who can traverse the most extreme distance in less than an instant.

Even up there near Alpha Centauri, you could praise and feel the presence of God.

During Mass, especially at the moment of Consecration, we are higher than any astronaut. We're somewhere they can't go with a satellite or space shuttle. We're in a different time-space continuum because we're in a spiritual dimension, with a window to eternity.

It's a priceless opportunity. It's what life is all about: getting in touch with God. Thanking Him. Getting in touch with His tranquility. Getting in touch with His Mercy.

Lamb of God Who takes away the sins of the world....

With those words how the graces flow! How then are we humbled! How then are we receivers on the wavelength of God! The speed of light may be 185,000 miles a second, but it's sluggish compared to the grace of God.

On the moon, we could call upon Him. We could call upon Him from Mars. We could call upon Him from the rings of Saturn. We could call upon Him from the barren rock of Pluto or Jupiter.

During Mass, we travel farther than anything in the galaxy because we are traveling to a spiritual dimension. A place where space and time have no relevance.

They say that in the afterlife there isn't a past or present. There are no centuries. There are no decades. There are no weeks or months. Everything is now. I don't pretend to understand how that can be, but I know that with earthly minds we're of very limited knowledge.

I also know there is no true wisdom, no true perception, no true perspective, without God. I know that the greatest infusions of knowledge come not from textbooks or chalkboards but during prayer, especially prayer said in conjunction with the Eucharist.

This is when we understand. This is when we begin to know—and appreciate—the vastness of our God.

When we're in touch we God, life becomes a joy; without Him there is only emptiness—a vacancy not unlike the dark regions of our universe.

It would be better to lose the sun, said Padre Pio, than the illumination of the Eucharist.

"One thing alone sustains me, and that is Holy Communion," said Sister Faustina. "From it I draw my strength; in it is all my comfort. I fear life on days when I do not receive Holy Communion. I fear my own self. Jesus concealed in the Host is everything to me. From the tabernacle I draw strength, power, courage, and light. Here, I seek consolation in time of anguish."

It's God we should be seeking, not some new means of space travel. It is only through God, it's only through the Holy Spirit and Christ, that we'll understand the nature of the universe. "Hidden Jesus, my purest love, my life with You has begun already here on earth," prayed Sister Faustina. "And it will become fully manifest in the eternity to come."

Blessed Faustina encountered her share of Eucharistic "miracles." She once reported how, when receiving Communion, she noticed in the cup "a Living Host." One of the Hosts seemed to be alive! When she asked why only one was imbued with animation, the Lord replied, *"I am the same under each of the species, but not every soul receives Me with the same living faith as you do, My daughter, and therefore I cannot act in their souls as I do in yours."*

God acts when we have faith. He gives signs to the believer more than to the skeptic. He looks for trust.

Once, during Consecration, with his own eyes, St. Gaspar Del Bufalo saw gold coming from the chalice. Chains of gold. Heavenly gold. A flow of precious metal. It must have meant something personal to him. I'm not sure what it symbolized. All I know is that St. Gaspar had believed. He had trusted. Now God gave Him a visible representation of His power, as He also did on Easter Sunday in 1171, to churchgoers at St. Mary of the Ford in Ferrara, Italy. They watched in shock as a stream of blood came from the consecrated Host when it was broken in two, and more incredibly, the Host itself seemed to turn to flesh.

It was like the awesome miracle of Lanciano. It was like so many other times—so many!—when Heaven has reminded us of the Eucharistic reality by manifesting blood. It reminds us of the blood that spotted a Host during 1317 in Hasselt, Belgium, or the Host that turned bloody in Siena, Italy, that same century. It reminds us of the blood that has appeared on Hosts in France and Germany.

"I cannot doubt at all Your Presence in the Eucharist," said St. Teresa of Avila. "You have given me such a lively faith that when I hear others say they wish they had been living when You were on earth, I laugh to myself, for I know that I possess You as truly in the Blessed Sacrament as people did then, and I wonder what more anyone could possibly want."

Incredibly, Eucharistic miracles are such today that there will soon be too many to recount. As with anything, we must await rulings of the Church with obedience. We must await verification. And whatever we may feel, we must be obedient to the local Bishop. Let me give one recent example. In February of 1996, at the Mission Church of Holy Family in Barbeau, Michigan, it was reported that a consecrated Host in an ablution cup next to the tabernacle began to change color. It had been placed there for dissolution because a Eucharistic minister had dropped it during Mass, but instead of dissolving in the water, strange things began to happen. A week after it was first placed in the cup, the Host appeared to be turning red. There was a dime-sized spot on the Host. Soon, it grew and darkened. "Believe me, I have placed many a Host in ablution cups over the years and never have I experienced anything like this," reported the pastor, Father Mark A. McQuesten.

While the Bishop worried that it might be a simple case of fungus (which has happened in some cases), the Host was soon engulfed in "blood-red liquid which prevented us from seeing much detail. The dish was completely crimson red," claimed Father McQuesten. Within three weeks the Host's appearance was "fleshlike," according to the priest. It looked like a gleaming red heart with darker red in the middle.

Still fearful that it might cause untoward effects, however, his Bishop ordered the Host disposed. When Father McQuesten went to follow those orders he says the sensation was almost overwhelming. It not only looked like flesh but felt like it too. "I had to tear the Host and break it into pieces," he said. "I had to flee the sacristy for the touch was too real. It was as though I had placed my hand into His side and my fingers into the nail prints in His hands. My Lord and my God!"

It was the Bishop's discernment that nothing sensational should consume his flock, and so he ordered the Host disposed. We must respect that decision. But I mention it as an example of all the reports. Something supernatural afoot. There are too many reports to deny them all. The photos from various parts of the world are remarkable. If only a small percentage are true, that amounts to a substantial number of occurrences.

And when authentic, these signs are obviously of significance or else God would not send them. He wants us to know that Mass is not a superstition. It's not an idle fantasy. It's not just a ritual. Whatever the veracity of particular cases, the Blood of Christ is indeed present in every Host.

Chapter 10

And with that Presence, our prayers become increasingly powerful.

Our prayers are powerful for the sick and the hungry. They're powerful for world peace. They're powerful for the deceased and for the Church and for the priesthood. They're powerful for our families. *Lord, hear our prayer.*

When we meditate on the Real Presence of Christ, when we know through simple faith that He is really there, that He is actually manifest, that He is really listening, our prayers reach a new level of force.

We are given an opportunity to hand up our own private petitions during Mass and this is a unique opportunity to address our most urgent needs. It's a moment that shouldn't be missed. It's a special channel to God. The Mass was instituted to draw us into one Body, praying for each other, and we're our brothers' keepers. We are called to care about our neighbors as much as we care about ourselves. We're called to pray especially that we all remain "one Body, one Spirit, in Christ." We're called to heal and teach and comfort. We're called to reconcile. We're called to preserve our loyalty and unity. The prayers of our Canon go back to the fourth century and still preserve (as a priest so nicely put it), "the fragrance of that primitive liturgy, in times when Caesar governed the world and hoped to extinguish the Christian faith; times when our forefathers would gather together before dawn to sing a hymn to Christ."

As the Church has informed us through centuries of councils, the Mass is not a mere representation but actual reality. It is a real and visible sacrifice. It's a tribute, an offering. It preserves the sacred rites of ancient Jews but frames them in the context of Jesus. It perpetuates His memory until the end of time and is applied for the sins we commit on a daily basis. It's an ongoing re-present-ment of His sacrifice on the Cross and also a celebration of His Resurrection.

The Catholic Church is both a joyful and suffering Church. During the Eucharist we travel with Jesus to Calvary. We are at the foot of the Cross with Mary, John, and the pious women. Jesus' wounds are our wounds and our wounds are His. We are in union. We are one Body. With that unification, and only with that unification, comes the Holy Spirit.

With it also comes Our Blessed Mother. She is stand-ing next to the tabernacle. You see a statue of her, along with the Crucifix, in every conventional church. She always points to the Eucharist—she's a part of the Eucha-rist—because Jesus' Flesh was her flesh. It came from her flesh just as His Blood came from her vessels. In con-junction with the Holy Spirit He took His Flesh from Mary.

That's why at many of the most famous Marian shrines you find special devotion to the Eucharist. She is "Our Lady of the Blessed Sacrament." She embodies the Mass. She was present for the major events in Jesus' life just as we are now present during the liturgy.

She points to the Eucharist and the Holy Spirit. When we feel the power of Mass, we're feeling the Holy Spirit. Just as He was the Spouse of Mary, so is the Holy Spirit Spouse of the Church. During Mass we should ask that the Holy Spirit be present in ourselves and our families. We should ask Him to touch the priest. We should ask Him for a special descent upon the entire congregation. When we invoke Him, He lifts us to a new and clearer level of perception. He opens our eyes. He clarifies. It's extremely important to see and move with the Holy Spirit, for when we don't, we fumble and miscalculate. We lack discernment. We act prematurely. Or we head in the wrong direction. We know the Spirit is around when we sense peace and joy.

Another word for it is "grace," and we should never move ahead of it. We should never move too fast. We should never jump the gun on grace, making decisions without it. We must beseech the Holy Spirit for everything, because when we do He guides us and teaches more direct prayer.

Ask the Holy Spirit to tell you what you need and how to pray for it!

Come Holy Spirit. Come Holy Spirit.

It is the Holy Spirit Who grants guidance, heals sickness, strengthens our bodies, and protects us against all untoward events. It's the Holy Spirit Who imbues Mass with Christ's Presence. When there are miracles or revelations, these are accomplished through the Holy Spirit. During Mass He is especially strong. He is especially willing to pervade our spirits. And we should invite that. We should beg for His arrival. We should beg Him to pray through our own minds and lips. Again, we should ask Him to reveal to us what it is we should be praying about.

He is the Spirit of Truth. He is the Spirit of prayerfulness.

When the priest gives us the opportunity to reflect upon our sins, we should ask the Holy Spirit to tell us what sins we most need to purge. We should ask Him to inspire our memories. We should ask Him to reach deep into our pasts and expunge any evil. We should ask the Holy Spirit to enlighten us as to what we need for spiritual development.

And we should cover ourselves with the whiteness of His protection.

Such is crucial in our time, when evil spirits are more numerous than ever, when they continue to climb in a horde from the pit, when they antagonize and anger and divide us. We need special protection, and that protection is given by the Holy Spirit. He draws us to the Father. He draws us to Jesus. As part of the Holy Trinity, He has the power to grant us health (if such is the Will of God) and shield us from demonism.

At Mass we should ask the Holy Spirit to protect us and our loved ones from accidents and disease. We should ask for protection from any unfortunate events. We should ask the Spirit to send special angels and further empower those we have. We should ask Him to guide our every thought and action. We should ask for a long, healthy life, a holy death, and the sure route to Heaven.

Nothing brings the Holy Spirit like the Eucharist, and with God, anything is possible. Anything can change. Anything can be accomplished. As the Virgin of Medjugorje once said, "*The most important thing in the spiritual life is to ask for the gift of the Holy Spirit. When the Holy Spirit comes, then peace will be established. When that occurs, everything around you changes. Pray for the Holy Spirit for enlightenment. Ask the Holy Spirit to renew your souls, to renew the entire world. Raise your hands, yearn for Jesus because in His Resurrection He wants to fill you with graces.*"

When that happens, when we have the Holy Spirit, then, according to Our Blessed Mother, we have everything.

Chapter 11

We also have the ability, through Christ, to send His power to others. As it says in Canon 3 of Church law, "If anyone says that the Sacrifice of the Mass is merely an offering of praise and of thanksgiving, or that it is a simple memorial of the sacrifice offered on the Cross, and not propitiatory (gaining God's favor), or that it benefits only those who communicate; and that it should not be offered for the living and the dead, for sins, punishments, satisfaction, and other necessities: let him be anathema."

In other words: the Mass is so potent it operates on many levels. It can have a tremendous effect on our lives. It can have an enormous effect on those we pray for. So it's important to extend the Holy Spirit to others. It's important to give as we receive. It's important to become a channel of the Spirit. We should pray blessings on everyone. We should pray blessings on our priests and nuns, who are under particular harassment. We should pray for the Vatican. We should pray for our bishops and their union with Rome. We should pray for everyone and everything that touches our existence.

At Fatima the Angel of Peace asked Lucia, Jacinta, and Francisco to make acts of Adoration and reparation to the Holy Trinity in the Blessed Sacrament. He asked them to offer up sacrifices to the Lord in order to erase the sins by which He was so offended—and thus to bring peace to that country. The angel held the chalice aloft with a Host suspended above it—with drops of blood falling from the Host into the chalice—and three times repeated this powerful prayer:

> *Most Holy Trinity, Father, Son, and Holy*
> *Ghost, I adore You profoundly and I offer*

> *You the most precious Body, Blood, Soul,*
> *and Divinity of Jesus Christ, present in all*
> *the tabernacles of the world, in reparation*
> *for the outrages, sacrileges, and indifference*
> *by which He Himself is offended. And by the*
> *infinite merits of His Most Sacred Heart and*
> *the Immaculate Heart of Mary, I beg of You*
> *the conversion of poor sinners.*

The Angel of Peace next gave the Host to Lucia and the chalice to her cousins Francisco and Jacinta, saying, *"Take and drink the Body and Blood of Jesus Christ, horribly outraged by ungrateful men. Make reparation for their crimes and console your God."*

The Fatima visionaries were also taught to say the prayer, *"Oh my Jesus, forgive us our sins, save us from the fires of Hell, lead all souls to Heaven, especially those most in need of Thy Mercy."*

In this time of grace, we should likewise offer up many supplications in order to prevent worldly chastisement. Instead of waiting for spectacular prophecies to unfold, we're called to pray that mankind avoid unpleasant circumstances. We're called to *prevent* chastisement. You see, when God gives prophecy, and when it is not just the idle imagining of the subconscious or a ruse of the devil, such a prophecy is to show us what would happen if God chose to exercise His judgment at that particular moment. It shows us the possibilities. It serves as a fruitful warning. Scripture tells us that prophecy is a vital gift (*1 Corinthians* 14:5). The reason for prophecy is to spur us into prayerful action, and in recent years we have heard so many dire prophecies that surely we have an easy time knowing what we are called to pray for!

We need to pray for morality. We need to pray that the Holy Spirit descend upon the world and lift its spiritual blinders. We need to pray that the terrible images coming out of Hollywood are halted. We need to pray for the morality of our leaders. We need to pray for an end of the culture of death: abortion, euthanasia, and things like RU-486 (the abortion pill). We need to pray for an end to all the negative images present in our society: the demonic cartoon characters, the influx of occult magic, the children's toys fashioned to look like devils. We need to pray for an end to the rampant drug use and the widely condoned promiscuity. We need to pray for deliverance from the pervasive materialism. And from the over-reliance on science (instead of on our Creator). We must urgently pray for reformation of the educational system and an end to a culture that so closely resembles the last days of Pompeii. More than anything, we need to offer up special petitions for our poor young people, who are so confused by what comes across television or what they hear in school that they can no longer distinguish between right and wrong, good and evil.

These young people are currently exposed to profanities that could only be imagined in the direst of prophecies ten years ago. Currently there are even trading cards and board games in which "fallen angels"—demons—are directly invoked. Some kids think it's "cool" to be possessed!

By the time the average American youngster is 13, he or she has witnessed thousands of murders and other acts of violence on television. The same is true of sexual activity. Soap operas are now to the point of pornography, and curse words are delivered to us during sporting events and talk shows in prime time. No wonder our young people are confused! No wonder, in some inner-city groups, the majority of births are now to unwed mothers.

These are things we need to pray about during Mass. These are issues we should bring to the altar. These are issues we should remember during Mass, which, as a representment of Calvary (as well as the Resurrection), has an enormous power to expel evil.

A single Mass is of immeasurable potency. St. Teresa explained that the world would long ago have been destroyed but for the Mass. It alone holds the arm of God. It alone restrains divine justice.

Without Mass in the world, said St. Teresa, "all here below would perish."

A single, well-said Mass—attended to with true grace—can have unimaginable effects. Our requests and supplications can be offered throughout the liturgy, and I have found it especially effective to do it while the Host is elevated, and also when the chalice is raised. For in the chalice is now the Blood of Christ, and it is that Blood which is most powerful in washing away sinfulness. It is the Blood which was shed for our redemption. It is the Blood that demons fear more than anything, because the Blood established Christ's transcendence of the world and defeat of evil. It represents His sacrifice. Since our redemption means breaking the bondages to Satan, the Blood is extremely potent in chasing away evil spirits.

During Mass we should plead the Blood of Christ. We should plead it on our lives. We should plead it on family and friends. We should plead it upon the Church. And society. We should plead it upon every aspect of existence because the Blood is the greatest of all palliatives—meaning that in warding off devils, nothing is more effective.

It was the Blood that defeated Satan at Calvary.

"Lord I am not worthy to receive You, but only say the word and I shall be healed...."

These are the cherished moments of Mass. These are the minutes that are special beyond our ability to understand how special they are. These are the seconds when we are touching eternity.

Having interceded for ourselves, our families, and the world, we have cleared the way to concentrating on our purification, and that opens the floodgates of grace, which pour forth during the Eucharist.

Upon reception of the Communion Host, we are in Christ and Christ is truly within us. Upon receiving Communion, we have all power over the enemy. As one of the documents from Vatican II proclaimed: "From this it follows that every liturgical celebration, because it is an action of Christ the Priest and of His Body, which is the Church, is a sacred action surpassing all others. No other action of the Church can equal its efficacy by the same title and to the same degree (SC 7). From the liturgy, therefore, and especially from the Eucharist, grace is poured forth upon us as from a fountain, and the sanctification of men in Christ and the glorification of God to which all other activities of the Church are directed, as toward their end, are achieved with maximum effectiveness" (SC 10).

Chapter 12

Yet until 13 years ago, I had no real idea of that. I had no understanding of the power. The word "grace" meant little to me. As I have previously written, back then I was a nonfiction author living in New York and had been away from the Church for quite a while as I wended my way through the modern system.

When I went to Mass for Christmas, Easter, or a wedding, it seemed like a dry, tedious ritual.

I wasn't alone. In fact, the majority of people my age, "baby boomers," had wandered away from regular church attendance. More than fifty percent. Much of the reason is society's fault, but part is also the fault of those who have stripped religion—including the Mass—of its mystical elements.

In an era of science, the supernatural had become a taboo subject. It became old-fashioned and "un-hip" to believe in a spirit world. *Superstitious*. And bowing to that pressure—trained in seminaries where the emphasis was suddenly more on science and philosophy than on Christian mysteries—priests were apprehensive about discussing subjects like miracles and the Virgin Mary.

There was no more mysticism. There were no more charisms. It seemed like signs and wonders were a thing of the past and homilies began to sound like college lectures.

There were words—dry theological words—but no discernible vigor.

I heard nothing about the dangers of the occult. I heard little about premarital sex. I knew nothing about the workings of Satan.

That this could happen shows us the disorientation of

modern times. And it was doubly confusing because the Church is founded on Jesus and He was no academic. He wasn't a dry scholar. He certainly didn't put his listeners asleep. He didn't stand at a chalkboard and expound upon pedantic details.

No, Jesus was a mystic. He was a worker of miracles. And it was those miracles—manifestations of the Holy Spirit—that convinced the people around Him that He was indeed the Son of God—a figure of unique transcendence.

Christianity was born as a result of His miracles and Spirit.

Yet somehow, for me, that Spirit was missing. I hadn't gotten much out of Mass until my conversion in 1983. It was then that I realized the liturgy is not just an ancient ritual, not just a cultural artifact. Suddenly I understood that I was not getting anything out of Mass because I wasn't putting enough *into* it. I was spiritually blind. It wasn't all the Church's fault. The Spirit wasn't moving because of my own sinfulness.

And lack of faith.

But once I returned, I was amazed: the power just exuded from everything about the Eucharist. I could feel anxieties and tensions dissolve when the Host was raised. I felt so much better after receiving Communion. I felt washed after Confession. I felt the devil lose his grip, especially when I looked up at the Stations of the Cross after Confession. The Mass seemed to focus on the Last Supper and Crucifixion until the hosts were consecrated. After that, joy flowed and there was the sense of Resurrection. There was a tangible feeling of the afterlife. What a supreme moment is the Eucharist! What power in the *Lord's Prayer!* What sweetness in the term "Lamb of God." I could feel a calmness when I received the consecrated wafer. I could taste the heavenly grace.

And I could feel the precious roots of Mass, the incredible way it had survived for 2,000 years, from the Last Supper and the first Eucharistic celebrations described around the year 150 by Justin Martyr to the increased reverence for the Eucharist during the Classical period and on to the Middle Ages.

Ours is an authentic Church built on glorifying God, as well as the rock of Peter.

"From age to age You gather a people to Yourself," we say at Mass, "so that from east to west a perfect offering may be made to the glory of Your Name."

Nothing brought me to a spiritual high like praising the Lord, like adoring Him, like sending Him love. There is such joy in loving God and that's the essence of Mass: giving God and Jesus and the Holy Spirit Their due praise. During the *Gloria*, we are hearkening back to the ancient hymns in the Church, assembled in the Holy Spirit to praise and appeal to the Father and the Lamb of God. This is a constant theme throughout the Eucharist. We are praising God as with the angels (*Luke* 2:13): *"Glory to God in the highest, peace on earth to those on whom His favor rests."* We worship God. We give Him thanks. We praise Him for His glory!

"For You alone are the Holy One, You alone are the Lord, You alone are the Most High."

And to the Lamb Who takes away the sins of the world, we ask mercy and reception of our prayer.

"You alone are the Most High, Jesus Christ."

He is with the Holy Spirit in the glory of God the Father.

And so we should add our own praise. We should let our hearts lift in love to Him Who is the King of all kings. Praise Him from our homes and from the rooftops of the cities, from the highest mountain, from the lowest valley, from the happiest and saddest moments in our lives. Praise You, oh Lord, praise You, Lord Jesus Christ!

In praising Christ we bless God and we ask for His blessing. The same is true when we bless ourselves. We are wrapping our entire bodies in the Body of the Lord when we make the Sign of the Cross. It's the holiest of all signs. It has great power of protection. We also use the special threefold Sign of the Cross, doing so on our forehead, mouth, and heart.

This is very significant. This is vital. For in so doing, we're invoking Christ to purify and seal our very essence.

Blessing our heads is important because we have to watch everything we think, lest evil thoughts take root.

49

They're like weeds, and unless we immediately halt a negative or evil thought, it plants itself and like crab grass begins to spread. It's not a sin to have an evil thought. They are often sent to us by the devil as temptations. But it *is* a sin to dwell on them. It's a sin to take hold of a sinful thought—a lustful, violent, hateful, or otherwise negative thought—and let it send forth its tendrils. We must bless our heads so that the only thoughts we have will be ones that are inspired and guided by the Holy Spirit.

We pray that pride, jealousy, and hatred never enter our contemplation.

"Take the helmet of salvation," says *Ephesians* 6:17.

The same is true of the mouth. We bless our lips so that nothing will come forth to sully us and drag us to the pit. As Christ said, it's not what we take in our mouths that defiles us but rather what comes *out* of our mouths (*Matthew* 15:11).

When we say negative things about others, however righteous we believe ourselves to be, we are passing judgment and we're told not to judge others (*Matthew* 7:1), or we will be judged by the same measure.

As much as we criticize and judge, so we will we be criticized and judged.

As much as we see the evil in others, so will the Lord see our evil.

From the lips come gossip and bickering and slander. These are serious transgressions, for when we bicker or slander, which means to detract from or discredit somebody, we are in league with Satan who is the original accuser and slanderer. Bickering leads only to division. Time and again Scripture warns about speaking ill of others, and mentions wrongful talk in the same breath as fornication (*Ephesians* 5:4-5). *"Get rid of all bitterness, all passion and anger, harsh words, slander, and malice of every kind,"* says *Ephesians* 4:31-32. *"In place of these, be kind to one another, compassionate, and mutually forgiving, just as God has forgiven you in Christ."*

We must bless our mouths because as the Bible warns, the tongue is a nearly inconceivably powerful member. *"See how tiny the spark is that sets a huge forest ablaze,"* says James 3:5-6. *"The tongue is such a flame. It exists among our members as a whole universe of malice. The tongue defiles the entire body. Its flames encircle our course from birth, and its fire is kindled in Hell."*

Thus we see how vital it is to bless our lips, and also our hearts, for as Scripture adds, slander and hate and lust originate in the heart. When we bless our hearts, we are inviting God's great purifying force to make us clean from the roots up. We are purging the seeds of evil and uniting our heart with that of Christ, showing the deep meaning behind blessing ourselves and every other aspect of Mass.

That's what I began to learn when I converted. That's what I got out of Mass once the Holy Spirit moved in. The very way in which we pray during Mass bears great significance, for when we do so with raised and extended hands, which is known as the "stance of the orantes," we are praying like the ancient figures who are depicted in the catacombs.

The extended arms remind us of salvation because they remind us of the Crucified Lord.

Chapter 13

With Christ, there are many hidden powers.

I remember how, after my conversion, I would roam around a church and wonder at the many obscure images—in stained glass, on altar carvings, or statues—that I'd never really noticed.

Such images of saints and other holy figures are to invoke the spirit of Heaven and the atmosphere of celestial existence. They can be crucial in placing us in a prayerful mood, although many Protestants misunderstand their value. They think statues represent "idolatry" when in reality the Bible speaks of idols as snakes and man-beasts—not angels or saints.

We have statues for the same reason that we have family photographs: to remind us, to create a reflective atmosphere. According to tradition, holy images were painted long ago, long before the Protestant rebellion, by the likes of St. Luke. The earliest miracles associated with a statue date at least as far back as the fourth century.

Then we have sacramentals such as holy water that ward off evil spirits. I often suggest that people use holy water daily and also blessed salt. Holy salt is a forgotten sacramental that's especially powerful against the devil. It can be mixed with water or sprinkled by itself.

The same power can come with holy images. Take the Shroud of Turin. One has to visit the vault to appreciate its power. It's kept at the Cathedral of the Holy Shroud in Turin, Italy. The history of this primitive cathedral hearkens back to the third century, when Christian martyrs laid down their lives for Christ during the persecution unleashed by a tyrant named Decius. The first bishop of Turin was St. Maximus, who was determined to put down rising heresies and pagan superstitions.

I'm not sure when the first cathedral was built. It was actually formed by joining three churches. One was dedicated to St. Mary Major, one to John the Baptist, and the third to the Holy Savior. Those churches were demolished in 1490, and the cornerstone for a new cathedral was laid in 1491. Obviously, there have been many additions and renovations since that time.

But I describe all this because the essence of Mass is to be found in this old cathedral, this stone monument that is now in the heart of a bustling Italian city. Over the entrance is a huge reproduction of DaVinci's "Last Supper," depicting the very origin of Mass. There are beautiful chapels dedicated to the Madonna and the Archangel Michael, along with breathtaking candelabra and marble statuary. In one side chapel is a most authentic crucifix, surrounded by figurines and sweeping statues of St. Teresa and St. Christina. At the main alter are towering candles and a transcending crucifix on the tabernacle.

And above that, behind tall and fortified glass, in an upper chapel reached by august and mysterious marble stairs, is the chapel of the Shroud and a monumental altar—a truly awe-inspiring altar—in which the cloth is kept.

It's like the Fort Knox of Catholicism.

And what better symbolism than the image of Christ above and behind the tabernacle!

There are splendid gold-plated angels around the iron grill of the Shroud's vault. In that is an asbestos-covered casket holding a silver chest containing the actual cloth. While the very sight of this chapel is enough to inspire the deepest reverence, it's nothing next to the spiritual feeling. As I stepped up to the encasement on short marble steps I suddenly felt a force bring me to my knees and the most comprehensive prayer imaginable flowed through my whispering lips—the best prayer I had ever prayed, covering all my needs and the direction of my life. I was as close as you can get, within a few feet of the actual Shroud.

While certain disbelieving scientists claimed, during the late 1980s, that carbon-dating indicated the Shroud is only 600 years old—which means it can't be the actual burial cloth—more recent studies indicate that such dating could have been off and that the cloth may indeed be nearly 2,000 years old. Recently I met a movie producer from Los Angeles who has worked with a team of experts to study the evidence for a major documentary. He said that not only did a re-evaluation of the carbon dating raise doubts about the previous tests, but like other researchers he raised the point that pollen found in the threads of the Shroud could only have come from certain plants found in the vicinity of Jerusalem and he claimed that one type of pollen has been extinct for 1,500 years, meaning the cloth is at least that old and comes from Israel.

To me the most important fact is not the age but the fact that no one can explain how such a detailed image got onto a piece of cloth. Even today we don't have such technology. The image was done in negative and only noticed for its extraordinary details in the 1800s, when the Shroud was first photographed and to the shock of the photographer, displayed a far more elaborate image than previously noticed with the naked eye. The details were hidden because the Shroud is actually like a film negative, and the details emerged only as film was being developed. It's inconceivable to me that a hoaxster could have anticipated photography centuries before it was invented and staged such a technological hoax.

I've seen much other evidence. But I don't really need any more. I know only this: when I approached the vault above the main altar, behind the tabernacle, I felt the Holy Spirit as I had rarely felt Him before.

I'll never forget the wonderful feeling, which for me symbolized the essence of the Eucharist. The peace. The strength of God. Pope John Paul II once said that "the Holy Shroud is a unique and truly providential sign of our times," and it gives us an image for the essence of the Eucharist. It reflects both Jesus and God. The very placement of a supernatural image of Christ in a city of spiritual warfare (there are many witches in Turin), and right above the altar, just over the tabernacle, is a sign of our times and tells us that when we partake of Com-

munion, when we swallow the wafer or drink of conse-
crated wine, we're touching the most powerful force in
Heaven. We're touching Jesus. We're touching His death.
We're ingesting His very power!

They speculate that an unknown force comparable to
the energy of an atomic blast left the image. That's what
we're in touch with. And there are signs of blood flow in
the Shroud, reminding us of what's in the chalice and the
fact that Christ's blood, like the lamb's blood at Passover,
protects us from the avenging angel.

The supernaturality of Communion was demonstrated
in Turin several centuries ago, when that city witnessed
its own Eucharistic miracle. The date was June 6, 1453.
According to writer Joan Carroll Cruz, two soldiers recently released from military service were passing through
the city of Exilles when they decided to pillage a church.
Gaining entrance, they collected candle holders, vest-
ments, and other expensive articles. Not yet content, they
went to the altar and removed the very ostensorium containing a large consecrated Host! Then they packed it all
up, plopped it on an unknowing mule, and headed for the
city of Turin. According to another account, they sold the
booty to merchants who traded the items (along with the
hapless donkey) among themselves.

That's when the miracle occurred. After entering the
city's gate the mule was beaten by one merchant and
suddenly stumbled and fell to the ground trying to dodge
the blows. "Everything packed on his back was jolted free
and scattered on the ground, including the ostensorium
containing the consecrated Host," wrote Cruz. "But the
Host did not fall. Rather, *it rose in the air, where it remained suspended amid splendid rays of light like a
heavenly sunburst*" (author's emphasis).

The event happened in front of a church site now
known as the Church of the Body of the Lord! And it was
witnessed by the Bishop himself, Ludovico of Romagnano,
who vested himself and rushed to the site, falling to his
knees in wonder before the levitated Host (which was suspended about 12 feet from the earth).

After worshipping the Host for an appropriate time,
the Bishop asked for a chalice and witnesses watched in

amazement as the Host descended into the chalice, as if lowered by unseen hands.

The miraculous Host was then taken to the church adjoining what is now the Shroud chapel, the Cathedral of St. John the Baptist, where it was known, due to its unearthly brilliance, as the "Sun of Justice."

I have not gone on like this for no reason. There is great significance to the sun. There is great meaning of the sun—as well as the concept of justice—in our own day. For the sun not only brings to mind other miracles where the Host has illuminated, it not only reminds us of other times when a Host has radiated visible power, but it also reminds us of instances, as at Fatima and Medjugorje, where there have been sun miracles.

The Miracle of the Sun, it turns out, is a sign of the Eucharist.

It's a sign of Adoration.

It's telling us to go to the chapel of the Blessed Sacrament and to do so without wasting any more time.

Chapter 14

For the charismatic movement is turning into a Eucharistic movement. The Marian movement is turning into a Eucharistic movement.

Our times are critical and the Sacred Heart is among us. He is granting special power. He is coming with the same overt grace that the Virgin has displayed at places like Fatima.

It is the time of the Eucharist. When we spend time in front of the Blessed Sacrament, we feel a power similar to that during elevation of the Host. We encounter a holiness second only to Mass. While nothing is more powerful than the liturgy, Adoration comes in second. During Adoration, which keeps the Blessed Sacrament right there before us, prayers are heard and answered.

I have spoken to nuns who have had visions of mighty angels in chapels of the Blessed Sacrament, and others who have encountered delightful and reverential strangers who in retrospect seemed like angels praying fervently before the Host or even prostrate on the floor of a chapel. In one shrine dedicated to Fatima in Youngstown, New York, a medical doctor reported the inexplicable materialization of a Host in the hands of a woman she was accompanying in the Blessed Sacrament chapel. Others saw or felt wonderful things while praying there, including an image of the Shroud that seemed to take shape in the monstrance.

If we could see just a fraction of the graces available before the Blessed Sacrament, we would flock to the nearest chapel each and every day. When I visit a church to deliver a speech, I can often sense when that church has Adoration of the Blessed Sacrament. I can sense it because there's a feeling of peace and unusually high Mass attendance. The Blessed Sacrament *draws* people. It imbues the church with an aura of holiness. It gives the parish an active charism. It becomes the very heart—the radiant and vibrant heart—of a parish.

St. Margaret Mary saw the Host this way, as radiant. Often, while praying before the Blessed Sacrament, it came alive to her. It served as a window—a port hole—into the heavenly dimension. It drew her like a powerful magnet. "I could have spent whole days and nights there, without eating or drinking, and without knowing what I was doing, except that I was being consumed in His presence like a burning taper, in order to return Him love for love," said St. Margaret Mary, speaking of the Blessed Sacrament.

It was there that St. Margaret Mary found a sense of safety. It was there that she got a taste of Heaven. And on the eves of Communion she found herself "rapt in so profound a silence"—simply by meditating on the greatness of the action she was about to take—that she could talk only with great effort.

After receiving Communion she felt such great peace and consolation that she wished neither to eat, drink, or speak.

One day, while praying before the Blessed Sacrament, St. Margaret Mary suddenly felt a strange sensation. It was as if she was being penetrated with the Divine Presence—to such a degree that she lost thought of herself and where she was. She had abandoned herself totally to the Holy Spirit, Who lifted her by the power of purity and love. It was then that she felt herself reposing in His grace and received the "inexplicable secrets of His Sacred Heart," which she later saw "as a resplendent sun, the burning rays of which fell vertically upon my heart."

This was the beginning of what would become one of the great devotions. This was the beginning of the Sacred Heart devotion.

On another occasion Jesus presented Himself to St. Margaret Mary in resplendent glory with His five wounds shining like little suns. "Flames issue from every part of His Sacred Humanity," she said, "especially from His adorable bosom, which resembled an open furnace and disclosed to me His most loving and most amiable Heart, which was the living source of those flames."

These flames will mean more when we discuss the flames of Purgatory. I've mentioned how Blessed Faustina had similar revelations. Many of them took place before the Blessed Sacrament. Once, in 1934, Faustina had a dream and during the vision she saw Jesus exposed in a monstrance under a big sky. Out of the Host came the same two rays that she saw coming from His Heart in the Divine Mercy image. This happened on other occasions as well: Sister Faustina seeing actual rays of light coming from the Blessed Sacrament. She described the rays as "bright and transparent like crystal," which is similar to how St. Teresa of Avila described Christ's Light as "not a radiance which dazzles, but a soft whiteness and an infused radiance." She compared it to looking at "a very clear stream, in a bed of crystals, reflecting the sun's rays."

I've already mentioned the radiance St. Margaret Mary saw, and many will recall that when Sister Lucia of Fatima saw Our Blessed Mother, she described the apparition as "more brilliant than the sun, shedding rays of light clearer and stronger than a crystal glass filled with the most sparkling water and pierced by the burning rays of the sun."

Indeed, after enough prayer the Blessed Sacrament—whether in a monstrance or elevated during Mass—seems to transform into a white luminosity. When the priest was blessing the people with the Blessed Sacrament, Sister Faustina saw the Lord and His rays over the whole world. "Jesus concealed in the Host is everything to me," she wrote in her diary. "From the tabernacle I draw strength, power, courage, and light. Here, I seek consolation in time of anguish. I would not know how to give glory to God if I did not have the Eucharist in my heart."

We remember Padre Pio saying that a few minutes before the Blessed Sacrament are worth more than years of any worldly endeavor.

No wonder so many saints spent hours before the altar—in some cases, as with St. Francis of Assisi, entire nights or days. One Holy Thursday, prostrate and without interruption, St. Margaret Mary spent fourteen hours in Adoration.

It is during Adoration that we get direction from On High. It's during Adoration that God speaks to us through the peace that touches our hearts. He speaks best not in locutions or visions but in the deep recesses of our consciousness.

The Eucharist serves as food for the soul and even the body. There is no scientist who would believe that the human body can be sustained by a little wafer of unleavened bread, yet it's said that St. Gerasimus of Palestine, who lived in the fifth century, subsisted on only the consecrated Host all through Lent.

In Switzerland during the fifteenth century was a hermit we know now as St. Nicholas of Flüe, who went twenty *years* without food. He said reception of the Eucharist once a month transmitted enough vital forces to keep his body functioning!

The mystic Anne Catherine Emmerich lived on water and the Eucharist for twelve years, and we also know that Therese Neumann received a number of miraculous Hosts—whereby the wafer would appear on her tongue without having been put there by a priest.

She existed with no food or water—only the Eucharist—for four decades (from 1926 until her death in 1962).

Unseen hands also conveyed the Eucharist to saints like Mary Magdalen de Pazzi, who died in 1607.

Most visual to me is the miracle said to have occurred to St. Catherine of Siena. While in ecstasy a hand of fire emerged holding a Host and placed it upon the saint's tongue.

In other cases we read accounts of demons who left the afflicted when they prayed before the Blessed Sacrament, or how exposition of the Host has supernaturally protected buildings and whole areas.

As Thomas á Kempis, author of *Imitation of Christ* wrote, "the Most Holy Sacrament, in union with the prayers of the saints, is able even now to heal the sick in soul and body."

Chapter 15

It is through the radiance, the fire of Jesus, that our sins are burned away. That's why so many envision fire falling from the sky. The Lord purifies with heavenly flames that issue from His Heart. They come from the furnace of His love. Our evil is evaporated in the Presence of Christ and is especially dispelled through Confession.

Confession prepares the way for the Eucharist and breaks the bonds of Satan. In verbally admitting our faults we are declaring a humility that immediately chases away Satan. He can not stand to be in our midst. He is the prince of pride. He cannot bear to stand in the presence of humility. He is powerless when a person is humble. He has no legal right to hold terrain.

When we confess sins we are renouncing sins, which means we are renouncing the devil. When we renounce the devil in the Name of Jesus, He has no choice but to leave. His chains are broken. His hold on our hearts and minds is lessened or expelled altogether.

During Communion, demonic infestations are often chased from our very bodies, or from around our families and friends.

The stronger a Confession, the more demonic residue is cleared.

The more demons that are expelled, the more peace.

That's why I said that before receiving Communion we should pray to the Holy Spirit to reveal any hidden faults we have never acknowledged and then take these to the confessional.

A good time for such soul searching is during Adoration. We should ask the Holy Spirit to allow us expiation of the slightest sins.

Go back to Scripture and note the many things that are listed by Paul as infractions, things we don't usually take to be of much consequence. Jealousy. Outbursts of anger. Selfishness. They're listed in *Galatians* with lewd conduct and sorcery (5:19-21)!

After we recollect all past transgressions—after we pray to heal all those we have ever hurt—we must maintain vigilance against repeating them. Confession should be a monthly ritual to keep ourselves pure, because when we are pure—when Christ has deigned to wipe clear the slate of those many sins—Communion and Adoration become all the more potent. They take on a special radiance. They sweep to the very bottom of existence and purge faults that will otherwise cause a long Purgatory.

There is nothing more enjoyable than the feeling of a spiritual cleanliness—nor is there anything more important for the soul's destiny. At least once a year, during Lent, we should prepare a special Confession and search for hidden faults that we have not previously realized. When we finally recognize that we've been doing something offensive to God—when we confess a sin that we had previously failed to notice—we are graced with inner peace.

That peace comes through liberation from past bondages. Communion becomes a powerful tool of deliverance. It's like the Lord snipping a rope that had been tying up a part of us. There's a feeling of strength and cleanliness. There's liberation. As Jesus said, *"If you live according to My teaching, you are truly My disciples; then you will know the truth and the truth will set you free"* (*John* 8:31-32).

To get that truth, we pray to the Holy Spirit. We ask Him to review our entire lives and bring to mind the best way of approaching Confession. During a Rosary, we let the Virgin take us through our personal histories and reveal anything hidden, anything obscure, anything forgotten. Most of us know the major sins, especially the Ten Commandments, but it's the more obscure sins, the "smaller" or venial sins, that often haunt us without our realizing it.

When we clear these, our Communion becomes all the more dynamic.

I've mentioned the sins of bickering, pride, and jealousy. Jealousy and pride are at the root of a tree that bears the bad fruit of division and negativity. The most common form of negativity is criticism. Exposing and criticizing a societal evil like abortion is one thing. We're *called* to expose something when we're certain it's from the evil spirit. We're called to correct society. But we must be very careful. If we point out failings without love, without sensitivity, that's not correction; it's criticism. And when we criticize someone, we're judging them.

We all know we're not supposed to judge (*Matthew* 7:1). To judge is to declare ourselves superior. To judge is to sound condescending. To judge is to somehow feel "above" the person or persons we're criticizing.

When we're jealous, it's all the worse. It's hostile. We're virtually wishing negativity upon those we're envious of.

And that's like sending a curse.

It's a "fiery dart" (*Ephesians* 6:16). It blinds us to our own faults and hinders our Eucharistic union.

When we receive Communion at the same time that we're harboring anger or unforgiveness or jealousy, we're not able to fully communicate. We're not in union with Christ's love and humility.

We're in a state of imperfection.

There's a blemish on our spirits.

And any such blotch thwarts the Holy Spirit.

Chapter 16

But just the opposite happens when we love. Just the opposite happens when we send good thoughts. Just the opposite happens when we wish another well, because when we have good thoughts we are sending a blessing.

And while we are blessing we're in communion with God.

When asked which commandment was the greatest, Jesus said, *"'You shall love the Lord your God with your whole heart, with your soul, and with your mind.' This is the greatest and first commandment. The second is like it; 'You shall love your neighbor as yourself.' On these two commandments the whole law is based, and the prophets as well"* (*Matthew* 22:37-39).

We are to love everyone. We are to send even our enemies blessings. Love is the energy, the medium, of Heaven. Without love, there is no Eucharist. Without love, there is little communication with Heaven. *"The man without love has known nothing of God, because God is love,"* says Scripture (*1 John* 4:8).

God sees love like we see a searchlight. He can spot love immediately. It's the defining quality of spiritual existence. It causes us to radiate. And it grows when we receive the Eucharist. It grows when we take Jesus into our hearts. It grows because Jesus is love and illumination.

That's why saints are pictured with a halo. It's an artistic rendering of a special glow that comes from a person who loves with the love of Christ.

When we love we are selfless. When we love we are blessing others. When we love our hearts are open and goodness pours forth. "After I have known it, LOVE works so in me," said St. John of the Cross, "that whether things go well or badly, LOVE turns all to one sweetness."

Or as St. Thérèse the Little Flower wrote to her superior: "How sweet is the way of love, dear Mother. True, one can fall or commit infidelities, but, knowing how to draw profit from everything, love quickly consumes everything that can be displeasing to Jesus...."

St. Thérèse explained that "merit does not consist in doing or giving much. It consists in loving much." Especially, in loving God. When we die, we're judged first and foremost on how much we have loved. Even sinners have found last-minute refuge because despite their serious transgressions, they had loved.

Hatred stirs up strife, says *Proverbs* (10:12), but love covers all sins.

We may fall, we may make a mistake, but love knows how to draw profit from all. It quickly consumes anything that may be contrary to Christ.

And it comes through the sacraments. It comes with Communion. "The Eucharist is the sacrament of love," explained St. Thomas of Aquinas. "It signifies love. It produces love."

It is a feast of love.

It is a vortex through which comes the affection of God.

As bread nourishes the body, so does Communion serve as food for the soul because it plants love. It nurtures love. It maintains love.

We need little else when we have the sacrament of love.

We're told by the saints that while on earth no one can properly appreciate the love and power of one Mass. As they say, it would be better for the sun to stop shining than for all Masses to come to a halt. The earth would plunge back into abysmal darkness. Mass is God's greatest gift to us. No one can comprehend its value because its value is infinite. "One merits more by devoutly assisting at a holy Mass than by distributing all of his goods to the poor and traveling all over the world on pilgrimage," said St. Bernard.

Its greatness is predicated on love. Its greatness is in its representation of unselfishness. We must love Christ through the Eucharist and then extend that love to our fellow humans. The more we receive, the more we should give. It all comes back. Love attracts love. Every time we love someone, something good happens throughout the universe. Every time we love a person, we are poised to cause a chain reaction. When we're nice to somebody, when we show consideration, especially to a stranger, he or she is often nice to someone in turn, and then the third person also does something nice, and soon there is a domino effect.

Every time we send love, we set the stage for a beautiful turn of events—and we erase past incidents in which we sent dislike and even hatred. Every time we send love, we make up for a time in the past when we *failed* to send love. We make up for incidents of dislike, irritation, and impatience. We atone for ill thoughts. Think of all the people you've interacted with during your life and how many times you've felt aggravation. Count the times you're tempted to anger. Count the times someone irritates you, or that negativity enters your thoughts. Keep a mental log of the incidents. Count the times you honk your horn or insult someone under your breath. Count the times you think of someone as inferior or "dumb."

The most simple acts of aggravation are troublesome to God. He does not forget a minute of our lives. When we die we're made to feel the emotions we caused in every person we ever had contact with. Good and bad. It's all on record.

But I like to think that every time we love, every time we send out good feelings, we erase a time when we didn't love. Each blessing—each kind thought we think about someone—erases a past curse. If we bless people all day long, we eventually make up for all the times we've sent curses in the form of negative thoughts. We erase all the hatred or dislike we previously held in our souls, and there is that much less to purge in the afterlife.

Bless your family each morning. Bless your friends. Bless your neighbors. Bless those who share the road or highway or sidewalk with you. Bless those behind you and those ahead of you. Bless those at the office, or the convenience mart, or the restaurant and cafeteria. Bless those on the elevator. Bless your boss. Bless your co-workers. Bless those at the bank or the mall or the gas station—and even the aggravating person taking his or her time at the supermarket checkout. Think of the person who has been causing you anger or anxiety. Think of the person who dislikes you, or who is arrogant, or a fierce competitor. Think of the person who has been envious or negative—who has been throwing you fiery darts—and feel love for that person.

In prayer, love the person who is most difficult for you to love. Love him or her. Pray for such people. If you can love them, you can love all. You're on your way to loving *everyone*. Love flows to each person who crosses your path, and you develop much more benevolence.

Bless everyone around you all day every day and then you are the walking Eucharist. Then you are a personification of the Host. Then you are with Jesus. As Mother Teresa says, works of faith and love are always a means of bringing us closer to God. Faith is trust and trust brings us closer to Him. If we are close to God we spread joy to everyone around us. Such benevolence, especially in the way of charity, is what Mother Teresa calls "the key to Heaven."

We go to Heaven if we live an earthly life as if we are constantly before the Eucharist, which means as if we are constantly in the Presence of God.

Chapter 17

And that brings us to the afterlife. That brings us to the greatest secret of Communion. It brings us to the role of the Eucharist in attaining a happy eternity.

As we all know, there are three basic destinations: Hell, Purgatory, and Heaven. Only in a flawless state, only in a pure state, can we go directly to Heaven. We must be as pure as the driven snow. We must be as white as the Host. Even the holiest and most dedicated people we have ever met might well be in need of a little purging. To kneel in God's Presence and to see His indescribable Face requires a spotless soul. The *Catechism* tells us that Heaven is the place of saints and angels. It's the ultimate destiny. It's where the majority eventually—eventually—end up.

But to go there directly a soul must be in a perfect state of faith, love, and humility. Only without a single blemish are we worthy.

Only in a pure state can we enter into His Pure Presence. Heaven is God and God is love. To blend into Heaven we have to *be* love. We have to be Eucharistic. We have to be humility. At the evening of death, says the *Catechism*, that's what we'll be judged on. It says that Heaven is for those "who die in God's grace and friendship and are perfectly purified." All who are still imperfectly purified are indeed assured of their eternal salvation, adds the *Catechism*, "but after death they undergo purification, so as to achieve the holiness necessary to enter the joy of Heaven."

As the *Catechism* further points out, the Church has always honored the memory of the dead. It does this during Mass in what's called the *memento*. It's done so that, purified, the souls can finally attain the vision of God. The Council of Trent declared that "those detained in Purgatory can be helped by the faithful through prayers and other expiatory works" and above all by the Holy Sacrifice.

According to Our Blessed Mother at Medjugorje, we are in "full conscience" and aware "of the separation of the body and soul" at the moment of death. Those who have experienced clinical death but have been resuscitated often describe a feeling of leaving the body and hovering over it, able to watch the nurses and doctors trying to revive them. We're told by our great mystics and theologians that immediately upon death, immediately upon separation from the body, our entire lives flash before us. In a way that can't be understood while we're still bound to the earth, the free soul is able to see every single act he or she ever did and review each and every situation of life, feeling what others felt while they were around us. There is no earthly time in eternity, and so in just a second—in just a flash—an entire lifetime can be reviewed with exquisite and often excruciating detail.

"It does not come by a voice to be heard by the ear, but in a manner entirely spiritual," wrote the esteemed Dominican theologian Reginald Garrigou-Lagrange. "Intellectual illumination awakens all acquired ideas, gives additional infused ideas, whereby the soul sees its entire past in a glance. The soul sees how God judges, and conscience makes this judgment definitive. All this takes place at the first instant of separation."

We get the same from certain saints, as well as from those who have what they call "near-death" experiences: that upon clinical death they went through a "tunnel," encountered a being of perfect light and love—perhaps an angel, or even Jesus—and were shown details of their lives at an extraordinarily rapid rate and yet also in a way that was vivid and real. Even the emotions and feelings associated with the images are re-experienced. We go back to childhood and up through our entire lives—reviewing every single person who in any way entered our lives and how we dealt with them. Each act of love is a plus; each antagonism is the opposite.

"When the soul leaves the body it is as if it were lost in or, if I may say so, surrounded by God," wrote an anonymous nineteenth century French nun whose mystical insights were considered most profound. "It finds itself in such a bewildering light that in the twinkling of an eye it sees its whole life spread out and at this sight it sees what it deserves, and this same light pronounces its sentence."

At judgment, souls go where they belong. They go to a destination that seems in conformity with their level of purity or impurity. In the pure Light of God's wisdom, they are unable to deceive themselves any longer, and seeing themselves as God does, they place themselves at the level of purgation that they warrant. No one who has impurity would be able to stand in God's Light with great comfort. In other words, they concur fully with God's judgment. In His Light we view every choice we have made and the repercussions, good and bad, of every decision. According to the Virgin of Medjugorje, we will see how we have helped or hurt God's plan, and then we will know where we belong in the hereafter.

If we have led a dutiful life, and especially if we had a dedication to Mass and the Blessed Sacrament, the purgation is lessened because in taking Communion we have already accomplished much in the way of purification. Masses that we attend while alive are more powerful than those said for us afterward. Every single moment spent in Mass or at the Blessed Sacrament is credited to us.

What a joy for those who had such a devotion, because as one holy writer said, a single Mass is more acceptable to Almighty God than all the sighs and tears of the whole world put together.

During Mass it is God, a pure God, offered up to God.

A growing number of people say they have gotten a foretaste of their "life review" while praying before the Blessed Sacrament. I recently met a television cameraman from Pennsylvania who had such an experience, and he was in awe at how every little action he ever took—how he dealt with people, how he raised his children, his every action of every day—was brought up during the replay. At Medjugorje it was reported that an Italian man praying before the Blessed Sacrament in April of 1995 had a similar encounter. He was adoring Jesus when suddenly, with no initiative on his part, the "movie" of his life began to unfold before his eyes with incredible detail and reality. He saw events from childhood and completely forgotten scenes that bore hidden meaning. He saw things in a way he had never previously considered, as if viewing them through God's eyes. He saw the true meaning of his life and rejoiced in the good things and saw how God drew benefit even from his evil deeds. "God used the evil there had been in my life to bring me to Him, and I was a-mazed to see in what a marvelous way He had succeeded in leading me through evil as well as through good," he said.

If the soul is guilty, it is so weighted by its own faults and lack of love that it naturally gravitates toward Hell or Purgatory. Those who are condemned to Hell are those who no longer want to receive any benefit from God, who continue to revolt against Him, refusing His final mercy. They are the ones who refuse to give Him credit or have sinned against the Holy Spirit (*Matthew* 12:31). They deny, resent, and blaspheme Him even though they now realize that He exists as the true Creator.

We all know the descriptions of Hell from places like Fatima: a sea of fire, with people in the flames transformed into creatures that are half animal and half human.

The Madonna of Medjugorje has given similar visions. She said many go to Hell but the majority go to Purgatory. There are probably as many situations in Purgatory as there are in earthly life. Every Purgatory is different just as every life is different. In Purgatory there are situations that are hellish, at one extreme, and very close to Heaven at the other end of the spectrum. Some purgatories last just days or minutes; some last for centuries. In Purgatory there is the joyful realization that God and Heaven exist, but there is the solemnity of knowing it will take a while to get there.

Those with only lesser sins do not stay so long in Purgatory. They are delivered by a few well-said prayers—especially the Mass—as well as sacrifices. For that reason the purgatorial souls long for Mass. They beg that Masses be said for them. They would give anything for one liturgical memento. Some souls are detained until a Mass is

71

finally applied to them, and when it is, it comes as an incomprehensible relief.

They are relieved, elevated, and sometimes even released.

A simple prayer for a soul in Purgatory, especially the Way of the Cross, is like a cool glass of water to someone thirsting on a desert.

The same is true of sacrifice. We should sacrifice the little miseries of life for such souls.

And when we ourselves die, they will return the favor. They'll be there to assist us.

A Mass for them is so potent. It is especially powerful for souls who neglected Mass while in the world. They now know that time on earth is invaluable—every second. They now know, as Father Alessio Parente, a longtime associate of Padre Pio's, has said, that we shorten our Purgatory by every liturgy and win a high degree of glory. We receive the priest's blessing which the Lord ratifies in Heaven. We kneel amid a multitude of angels who are present with reverential awe at the adorable sacrifice.

Chapter 18

Lives lived without Mass and love for God are atoned for by intense sufferings in Purgatory. Some say a moment in Purgatory can be more difficult than the hardest life. Minutes are like years. There are flames there, too, we are told, and they make the hottest flame on earth seem like a cool breeze by comparison.

"In Purgatory there are different levels," says the Virgin of Medjugorje. *"The lowest is close to Hell and the highest gradually draws near to Heaven. It is not on All Soul's Day but at Christmas that the greatest number of souls leave Purgatory. There are in Purgatory souls who pray ardently to God but for whom no relative or friend prays on earth. God makes them benefit from the prayers of other people. It happens that God permits them to manifest themselves in different ways, close to their relatives on earth, in order to remind men of the existence of Purgatory and to solicit their prayers to come close to God Who is just, but good. The majority go to Purgatory. Many go to Hell. A small number go directly to Heaven."*

Many souls find themselves in Purgatory due to lust and pride. The sin of pride is the root of many other sins. Pride is self-centered and therefore the opposite of love. Pride is seeking power and attention. Pride is believing what we do is superior to the work of another. Pride is believing we are always right. Pride is conceit, haughtiness, and self-satisfaction. Pride is criticality. Pride is a puffed-up sense of self worth. Pride is when we do something—even something religious—for ourselves instead of the Lord.

When we do that we become blinded to our conceit and can't even *see* our arrogance.

This is very dangerous, because when we're arrogant—when we think we're better than others—we're doing spiritual violence to those we feel superior to. It is pride that inspires the miser. It's pride that inspires the tyrant. It's ethnic pride that starts so many wars. Pride leads to materialism and other offenses.

Offenses that send people to a purgation that is most painful.

As Christ told Sister Faustina, *"All these souls are greatly loved by Me. They are making retribution to My justice. It is in your power to bring them relief. Draw all the indulgences from the treasury of My Church and offer them on their behalf. Oh, if you only knew the torments they suffer...."*

It is the absence of God that creates the greatest suffering. In Purgatory, says Mary, there are even persons who have been consecrated to God—some priests and religious—whose intentions must be prayed for, and a large number of souls who have been there a long time because no one remembers them.

They thirst for Mass. They hunger voraciously for it. Knowing now what they know, they would give anything to be able to return to earth for one simple liturgy! Such is confirmed by revelations given to the French nun in the nineteenth century, revelations that were reviewed favorably as regards doctrinal truth by Canon Dubosq, who was *promotor fidei* in the beatification and canonization process of St. Thérèse the Little Flower. In language stunningly similar to that which would come out of Medjugorje a century later, the anonymous nun, who was also granted an *imprimatur* by Cardinal Lawrence Shehan of Baltimore, reported that there are indeed different degrees of Purgatory. "In the lowest and most painful, like a temporary Hell, are the sinners who have committed terrible crimes during life and whose death surprised them in that state," she said. "It was almost a miracle that they were saved, and often by the prayers of holy parents or other pious persons. Sometimes they did not even have time to confess their sins and the world thought them lost, but God, whose mercy is infinite, gave them at the moment of death the contrition necessary for their salvation on account of one or more good actions which they performed during life. For such souls, Purgatory is terrible. It is a real Hell with this difference: in Hell they curse God, whereas (in Purgatory) souls bless Him and thank Him for having saved us."

I have seen some very sobering descriptions of lowest Purgatory. It seems to be a place for those with grave sins, even sins as serious as suicide, but who had some merit and did not defame God. There really is no human way of understanding lower Purgatory—it's not a physical place—but in the literature of mystical theology are writers who have tried to capture its sufferings by describing it alternately as a place of fantastic, searing heat, or for others a place of unbearable cold and darkness.

"Next to these come the souls who though they did not commit great crimes like the others were indifferent to God," said the French nun. "They are in Purgatory for long periods of indifference. There are in this stage of Purgatory religious of both sexes who were tepid, neglectful of their duties, indifferent toward Jesus, also priests who did not exercise their sacred ministry with the reverence due to the Sovereign Majesty and who did not instill the love of God sufficiently into the souls confided to their care.

"In the second Purgatory are the souls of those who died with venial sins not fully expiated before death, or with mortal sins that have been forgiven but for which they have not made entire satisfaction to the Divine Justice.

"Lastly there is the Purgatory of desire which is called the 'threshold.' Very few escape this. To avoid it altogether, one must ardently desire Heaven and the vision of God. That is rare, rarer than people think, because even pious people are afraid of God and have not, therefore, a sufficiently strong desire of going to Heaven. This Purgatory has its very painful martyrdom like the others. The deprivation of the sight of our loving Jesus adds to the intense suffering."

We can't get directly to Heaven unless, during life, we demonstrate a tireless desire to be in Heaven with the Lord.

The most effective way of doing that is to spend time in Adoration before the Blessed Sacrament.

At Medjugorje the seers described one area of Purgatory as like a rainy day: gray and with fog. Souls cry out in pain but can't be seen. The dark is a living darkness. "Purgatory is like some sort of dark chasm, some dark space between Heaven and Hell," said the visionary Vicka Ivankovic. "It is filled with something like ashes and it looks awful! We could sense persons weeping, moaning, trembling."

The seer Marija said she saw people in Purgatory as immersed in deep clouds. "They are desperately in need of our prayers," she told one interviewer. "The Blessed Mother asks us to pray for the poor souls in Purgatory, because during their lives here, one moment they thought there was no God, then they recognized Him, then they went to Purgatory where they saw there is a God, and now they need our prayer. With our prayers we can send them to Heaven."

Those with insights into Purgatory have told us that we should practice perpetual Adoration in our hearts at all times and we should prepare for Communion by meditating beforehand. We must carefully prepare an abode for Christ—praying to Him before Mass—and also invite Him to remain with us by our love for Him. We must throw ourselves entirely into His divine arms, into His Sacred Heart, and then there is no reason for fear. If every morning we say a prayer to Our Lord and adore Him to make up for the Adoration that is lacking in so many churches—if we pray as if in abandoned chapels, making up for the emptiness in so many churches—how much we relieve Him and cause Him to want to make a special effort on our behalf when we need Him during our final hours!

Only if we adopt God's Will as our own, only if we rid our actions of self will and instead do everything for God, do we head toward the kind of perfection necessary to enter Heaven.

To do something through self will is self defeating. If there is a motive that involves self will instead of God's Will, we are not living the Eucharist, whereas if we live the Mass we are walking with Jesus to Calvary and thus to our own resurrection.

We best live God's Will through reception of the Eucharist.

That's when Jesus *communicates.*

That's when we get our bearings.

Chapter 19

And that's the final value of the Eucharist.

Attainment of Heaven.

In his book *Crossing the Threshold of Hope*, Pope John Paul II says the Eucharist and other sacraments create in man "the seed of eternal life." When we receive Christ in Communion we are exerting the ultimate faith in His ability to manifest among us, and opening the door to realization that it is Heaven and only Heaven we must aspire to!

Nothing else in life matters. The afterlife is all-important. It's the reason for life on earth, which is a test and preparation.

St. Margaret Mary said that a soul in Purgatory once appeared to her enveloped in fire and explained that the greatest cause for his suffering (he was a Benedictine) was that in life he had preferred his own interests to those of God. He had been overly attached to his good reputation. His second defect was lack of charity to his brethren, and a third was his all too natural attachment to creatures.

But after St. Margaret Mary prayed and suffered for that soul, he was freed of his bondage. She saw him radiant with joy and glory. He had finished his purgation.

Each time we receive Holy Communion, according to St. Gertrude, something good happens to every being in Heaven, on earth, and in Purgatory. The Curs de Ars once added that a Communion well received is worth more than a small fortune given to the poor. Each time we receive Communion our place in Heaven is permanently raised and our stay in Purgatory is shortened. While on earth, with limited vision, we will never be able to appreciate the greatness of the Eucharist. We will never be able to comprehend the real fact of reliving Christ's crucifixion.

But we know the importance from places like Medjugorje. *"Unceasingly adore the Most Blessed Sacrament of the altar,"* said Our Blessed Mother. *"Special graces are then being received. Be kind to come to Mass without looking for an excuse. Pray, pray, pray only. Prayer should be for you not only a habit, but also a source of happiness. Abandon yourselves to God without any restrictions. Love your enemies. Banish from your heart hatred, bitterness, preconceived judgments. If you knew what grace and what gifts you receive, you would prepare yourselves for (the Eucharist) each day for an hour at least. Pray, dear children, so that God's plan may be accomplished, and all the works of Satan be changed in favor of the glory of God. When I say 'pray, pray, pray,' I do not only want to say to increase the number of hours of prayer, but also to reinforce the desire for prayer, and to be in contact with God. Place yourself permanently in a state of spirit bathed in prayer. Dear children, I want you to comprehend that God has chosen each one of you in order to use you in a great plan for the salvation of mankind. You are not able to comprehend how great your role is in God's design. The Mass is the greatest prayer of God. You will never be able to understand its greatness. That is why you must be perfect and humble at Mass. I beseech you, pray to Jesus! I am His mother, and I intercede for you with Him, but everything does not depend solely on me, but also on your strength and the strength of those who pray. The Mass is the most important and the most holy moment in your lives. If you abandon yourselves to me, you will not even feel the passage from this life to the next life. You will begin to live the life of Heaven from this earth."*

In Heaven, according to the seers, there is beauty beyond beauty. There is music beyond earthly music. There is peace beyond earthly composure. In Heaven light seems to radiate from an object instead of reflecting off it, and everything is alive, and even the flowers sway as if singing praises to God. "The grass was of a beauty I can't describe," Mirjana once told an interviewer. "The flowers were so beautiful I can't describe them."

There are living waters, and there are pure spirits with perpetual smiles because they live in an environment of

God and love.

A key component of that purity is humbleness. They are humble and only when we're humble are we in close union with He Who was humility itself. Only with humbleness can we fully love.

Humility is a very major requirement of Heaven. It is something we must focus upon all the time. Humility is unselfishness. It's turning the other cheek. It's living a life of service to others. Humility is the opposite of pride, just as light is the opposite of darkness. Humility is selfless love. Humility is the Eucharist: plain and simple bread. Unleavened bread. Bread that is not puffed up.

"Let the greater among you be as the junior, the leader as servant," said Jesus (*Luke* 22:26-27). *"Who, in fact, is the greater—he who reclines at table or he who serves the meal? Is it not the one who reclines at table? Yet I am in your midst as the One Who serves you."*

When we too serve others, we're exercising love and humility. And when we focus on others, our own anxieties, our own vulnerabilities, instead of consuming us, are put into better perspective.

When we concentrate on the needs of others there is a diminishing of our own problems.

The Blessed Sacrament brings such humility because during Adoration we are loving God and forgetting our selves.

ॐ ✦ ॐ

I like to think of Heaven as a feeling akin to constant and eternal reception of the Eucharist. It's like receiving Christ twenty-four hours a day. It's like the highest point we have ever achieved, and then far higher. It draws me to think of times I've had extraordinary experiences, like the visit to Rome a few years back when, suddenly, although I had no ticket, I found myself moved by the crowd into St. Peter's Basilica one Sunday morning, and there I was—at a Mass being celebrated by Pope John Paul II.

There are many things you remember from a special Mass. You remember the great feeling that comes from the atmosphere. You remember the graces that pour upon so huge a crowd. But of all things I most remember the joy and at the same time the awesome seriousness on the face of John Paul when he raised the Host during the Consecration. The thousands packed in St. Peter's seemed to stop their very breathing. There was a great hush as the Pope spent quite a while displaying the Host first to one side, then to the front, then to the other side, and then to the back, so magnificently showing Christ in the Eucharist to everyone in the basilica—a huge, white, shining Eucharist, a Host that nearly seemed to radiate like some of those historic miracles, a Host that even in the darkest of dark, even in a time of great evil, radiates always and everywhere.

In the Blessed Sacrament, we experience a little piece of Heaven. Paradise manifests itself through the sacrament. It manifests in the way of peace. It manifests in the calm we feel after Communion. It manifests in the way of miracles visible and invisible.

Just as there were a flurry of Marian apparitions, now we also have a flurry of Eucharistic miracles. I think this is highly significant. People often ask what the future will bring. Well, I think we're going to experience a heightened presence of Jesus. We're going to much better appreciate Communion. We're going to see more force in the sacraments. There will be many signs, and a good number of them will come through the Eucharist. Jesus will radiate yet stronger. We will hear of many healed before the Blessed Sacrament.

This enhanced experience of the Eucharist will signal the reign of the Sacred Heart, and that's good news indeed. The reign of the Sacred Heart will spell the end of much evil. One day soon, it will spell the end of Satan's century. The Presence of Christ dispels the man of perdition (*2 Thessalonians* 2:8). It joins the Immaculate Heart in announcing victory. Jesus is even now arriving. His Heart will become more prominent and we will see more intervention. But first He must be called. He must be invoked. We must invite Him. So call. Invite Jesus. Call Him from the mountains, call Him from the rooftops. Call to Him in Adoration. Call that He take us to the Face of God and the Light of His Kingdom.

REFERENCES

It is Christ himself, the eternal high priest of the New Covenant who, acting through the ministry of the priests, offers the Eucharistic sacrifice. And it is the same Christ, really present under the species of bread and wine, who is the offering of the Eucharistic sacrifice.

[*Catechism of the Catholic Church*, 1410]

As sacrifice, the Eucharist is also offered in reparation for the sins of the living and the dead and to obtain spiritual or temporal benefits from God.

Anyone who desires to receive Christ in Eucharistic communion must be in the state of grace. Anyone aware of having sinned mortally must not receive communion without having received absolution in the sacrament of penance.

[*Catechism of the Catholic Church*, 1414-1415]

This means that whoever eats the bread or drinks the cup of the Lord unworthily sins against the body and blood of the Lord. A man should examine himself first; only then should he eat of the bread and drink of the cup. He who eats and drinks without recognizing the body eats and drinks a judgment on himself.

[*1 Corinthians* 11:27-29]

... [T]he Jews quarreled among themselves, saying, "How can he give us his flesh to eat?" Thereupon Jesus said to them:

Let me solemnly assure you, if you do not eat the flesh of the Son of Man and drink his blood, you have no life in you. He who feeds on my flesh and drinks my blood has life eternal, and I will raise him up on the last day. For my flesh is real food and my blood real drink. The man who feeds on my flesh and drinks my blood remains in me, and in him. Just as the Father who has life sent me and I have life because of the Father, so the man who feeds on me will have life because of me. This is the bread that came down from heaven. Unlike your ancestors who ate and died nonetheless, the man who feeds on this bread shall live forever.

[*John* 6:52-58]

Sister Faustina's quotes were taken from:

The DIARY of Sister M. Faustina Kowalska, Divine Mercy in my Soul (translated from the original Polish), copyright © 1987 Congregation of Marians of the Immaculate Conception; All world rights reserved; Printed with permission; Imprimatur: Joseph F. Maguire, Bishop of Springfield, MA., March 16, 1987.

Other Books by Michael H. Brown

The Trumpet of Gabriel

Society is currently fascinated with angels and other spiritual/supernatural phenomena. What does it mean? Many denominations report this as God's call for mankind to reform. Includes insights from Pat Robertson, Billy Graham, Fr. Stefano Gobbi, and Pope John Paul II. 320pp.

Order #7714 — $11.00   **ISBN: 1-880033-16-X**

Witness - Josyp Terelya
Autobiography of Josyp Terelya
Co-Authored By: Michael Brown

The dynamic autobiography of a contemporary mystic, suffering servant, and victim of Communism. Published before dramatic changes in Europe and the Soviet Union, it is a story of supernatural events and accurate predictions. 344pp.

Order #7715 — $12.00   **ISBN: 1-877678-17-1**

Final Hour

Akita, Betania, Fatima, Garabandal, Knock--all are obscure places on maps, or are they? Has the mother of Jesus appeared at these and other international locations? Why? Investigative journalist Michael H. Brown provides compelling information about our extraordinary century. This all time best seller includes a fascinating look at secular history and Biblical prophesies! Excellent photos. 368pp.

Order #7716 — $12.50   **ISBN: 1-57918-133-3**

After Life
What it's Like in Heaven, Hell, and Purgatory

What happens when we die? Journey from the moment of death to the eternal joy in store for those who follow Christ. Interviews with those who claim near-death experiences, Catholic and scientific literature, and historic accounts of the saints reveal fascinating glimpses of the afterlife. 120pp.

Order #7717 — $6.50   **ISBN: 1-880033-25-9**

Prayer of the Warrior

Spiritual warfare is at an all-time high! In whose army are you a member? A riveting account of front line action in the eternal battle between good and evil as experienced by best-selling author Michael H. Brown. Parapsychology, a brush with the Mafia, and fascinating encounters with the supernatural make Michael's story something you will not want to miss and inspires all to join in this spiritual war. 256pp.

Order #7711 — $11.00   **ISBN: 1-880033-10-0**

Seven Days with Mary

This is a book of devotion based on the most ancient and solid of Mary's historic apparitions. Mr. Brown takes one of Mary's approved appearances for each day of the week and explains its often hidden aspects and offers prayers and meditations to accompany it. 112pp.

Order #7713 — $6.50   **ISBN: 1-880033-26-7**